I0198069

THE AMERICAN SPELLING BOOK

Containing the Rudiments of the
English Language, for the
use of Schools in the United States

Context Publications

2019

First Edition

Printed in the United States of America

First Printing, 2019

ISBN 978-0-578-55054-1

Context Publications
165 Snow Rd
Bridgewater, ME 04735

www.contextpublications.com

For the last three years I have been studying the history of the education system in North America. In my studies I stumbled across The American Spelling Book. I purchased a facsimile copy of the book and read it and was amazed by what I found. The American Spelling Book was thorough, short, and simple. All of these qualities are absent in modern textbooks.

In 1782 Noah Webster was teaching school in Goshen N.Y. His experience teaching convinced him that the United States of America needed curricula that was uniquely American instead of the imported British textbooks he was using. In the winter of 1782 he began writing the American Spelling Book.

After completing the book he borrowed money from friends to pay for publishing the book. The book rapidly grew in popularity becoming the standard for textbooks in the United States. The book was used in North American schools for over 100 years. The last edition of the this book was printed in 1908. Over 100,000,000 million copies of The American Spelling book have been sold. The book has had a long lasting influence on American culture and American spelling. Most variations in British and American spelling can be traced to the American Spelling Book.

We reproduced this book because we were dissatisfied with the quality of the facsimile editions of the book and we felt the book was still useful as both a textbook and a record of America's past. We made as few changes as we could to the original text.

We made a few minor changes to the book to make it easier to use as a spelling book. The changes we made are:

• We modernized the typesetting and fonts.

• We updated the spelling of a few words.

• The revised book uses a larger page size. This makes the book easier to use as a textbook.

• Any updates, ideas, and historical background is available on our website at www. contextpublications.com

We hope you enjoy the book as much as we have.

Daniel & Laurel Livesey

Preface

THE AMERICAN SPELLING BOOK, or First Part of a Grammatical Institute of the English language, when first published, encountered an opposition, which few new publications have sustained with success. It, however, maintained its ground, and its reputation has been gradually extended and established, until it has become the principal elementary book in the United States. In a great part of the northern States, it is the only book of the kind used; it is much used in the middle and southern States; and its annual sales indicate a large and increasing demand. Its merit is evinced not only by this general use, but by a remarkable fact, that, in many attempts made to rival it, the compilers have all constructed their works on a similar plan; some of them have most unwarrantably and illegally copied a considerable part of the tables, with little or no alteration; and others have altered them, by additions, mutilations and subdivisions, numerous and perplexing. In most instances, this species of injustice has been discountenanced by the citizens of the United States, and the public sentiment has protected the original work, more effectually than the penalties of the law.*

Gratitude to the public, as well as a desire to furnish schools with a more complete and well digested system of elements, has induced me to embrace the opportunity when the first patent expires, to revise the work, and give it all the improvement which the experience of many teachers, and my own observations and reflections have suggested. In the execution of this design, care has been taken to preserve the scheme of pronunciation, and the substance of the former work. Most of the tables, having stood the test of experience, are considered as susceptible of little improvement or amendment. A few alterations are made, with a view to accommodate the work to the most accurate rules of pronunciation, and most general usage of speaking; as also to correct some errors which had crept into the work. A perfect standard of pronunciation, in a living language, is not to be expected; and when the best English Dictionaries differ from each other, in several hundred, probably a thousand words, where are we to seek for undisputed rules? and how can we arrive at perfect uniformity?

The rules respecting accent, prefixed to the former work, are found to be too lengthy and complex to answer any valuable purpose in a work intended for children; they are therefore omitted. The geographical tables are thrown into a different form; and the

---

* The sales of the American Spelling Book, since its first publication, amount to more than TWO MILLIONS of copies, and they are annually increasing. One great advantage experienced in using this work is the simplicity of the scheme of pronunciation, which exhibits the sounds of the letters, with sufficient accuracy, without a mark over each vowel. The multitude of characters in Perry's scheme render it far too complex and perplexing to be useful to children, confusing the eye, without enlightening the understanding. Nor is there the least necessity for a figure over each vowel, as in Walker, Sheridan, and other authors. In nine-tenths of the words in our language, a correct pronunciation is better taught by a natural division of the syllables, and a direction for placing the accent, than by a minute and endless repetition of characters.

abridgment of grammar is omitted. Geography and Grammar are sciences that require distinct treatises, and schools are furnished with them in abundance. It is believed to be more useful to confine this work to its proper objects – the teaching of the first elements of the language, spelling and reading. On this subject, the opinion of many judicious persons concurs with my own.

The improvements made in this work chiefly consist in a great number of new tables. Some of them are intended to exhibit the manner in which derivative words, and the variations of nouns, adjectives and verbs, are formed. The examples of this sort cannot fail to be very useful, as children, who may be well acquainted with a word in the singular number, or positive degree, may be perplexed when they see it in the plural number, or comparative form. The examples of derivation will accustom youth to observe the manner in which various branches spring from one radical word, and thus lead their minds to some knowledge of the formation of the language, and the manner in which syllables are added or prefixed to vary the sense of words.

In the familiar lessons for reading, care has been taken to express ideas in plain, but not in vulgar language; and to combine, with the familiarity of objects, useful truth and practical principles.

In a copious list of names of places, rivers, lakes, mountains, &c. which are introduced into this work, no labor has been spared to exhibit their just orthography and pronunciation, according to the analogies of our language, and the common usages of the country. The orthography of Indian names has not, in every instance, been well adjusted by American authors. Many of these names still retain the French orthography, found in the writings of the first discoverers or early travelers; but the practice of writing such words in the French manner ought to be discountenanced. How does an unlettered American know the pronunciation of the names, ouisconsin or ouabasche, in this French dress? Would he suspect the pronunciation to be Wisconsin and Waubosh? Our citizens ought not to be thus perplexed with an orthography to which they are strangers. Nor ought the harsh guttural sounds of the natives to be retained in such words as Shawangunk, and many others. Where popular practice has softened and abridged words of this kind, the change has been made in conformity with the genius of our language, which is accommodated to a civilized people; and the orthography ought to be conformed to the practice of speaking. The true pronunciation of the name of a place is that which prevails in and near the place. I have always sought for this, but am apprehensive, that, in some instances, my information may not be correct. It has, however, been my endeavor to give the true pronunciation in the appropriate English characters.

The importance of correctness and uniformity, in the several impressions of a book of such general use, has suggested the propriety of adopting effectual measures to insure these desirable objects; and it is believed that such measures are taken, as will render all the future impressions of this work uniform in the pages, well executed, and perfectly correct.

In the progress of society and improvement, some gradual changes must be expected in a living language, and corresponding alterations in elementary books of instruction become indispensable; but it is desirable that these alterations should be as few as possible, for they occasion uncertainty and inconvenience. And although perfect uniformity in speaking is not probably attainable in any living language, yet it is to be wished, that the youth of our country may be, as little as possible, perplexed with various differing systems and standards. Whatever may be the difference of opinion among individuals, respecting a few particular words, or the particular arrangement of a few classes of words, the general interest of education requires that a disposition to multiply books and systems, for teaching the language of the country, should not be indulged to an unlimited extent. On this disposition, however, the public sentiment alone can impose restraint.

As the first part of the Institute met with the general approbation of my fellow citizens, it is presumed the labor bestowed upon this work, in correcting and improving the system, will render it still more acceptable to the public, by facilitating the education of youth, and enabling teachers to instill into their minds, with the first rudiments of the language, some just ideas of religion, morals and domestic economy.

N.W.

NEW-HAVEN, 1803

ANALYSIS OF SOUNDS

IN THE

ENGLISH LANGUAGE.

LANGUAGE, in its more limited sense, is the expression of ideas by articulate sounds. In a more general sense, the word denotes all sounds by which animals express their feelings, in such a manner as to be understood by their own species.

Articulate sounds are those which are formed by the human voice, in pronouncing letters, syllables and words, and constitute the spoken language, which is addressed to the ear. Letters are the marks of sounds, and the first elements of written language, which is presented to the eye.

In a perfect language, every simple sound would be expressed by a distinct character; and no character would have more than one sound. But languages are not thus perfect; and the English Language, in particular, is, in these respects, extremely irregular.

The letters used in writing, when arranged in a certain customary order, compose what is called an Alphabet.

The English Alphabet consists of twenty-six letters, or single characters; and for want of others, certain simple sounds are represented by two letters united.

The letters or single characters are, a, b, c, d, e, f, g, h, i, j, k, l, m, n, o, p, q, r, s, t, u, v, w, x, y, z. The compound characters representing distinct sounds are, ch, sh, th. There is also a distinct sound expressed by ng, as in long; and another by s or z, as in fusion, azure, which sound might be represented by zh.

Letters are of two kinds, vowels and consonants.

A vowel is a simple articulate sound, formed without the help of another letter, by opening the mouth in a particular manner, and begun and completed with the same position of the organs; as, a, e, o. The letters which represent these sounds are six; a, e, i, o, u, y. But each of these characters is used to express two or more sounds.

The following are the vowel sounds in the English Language –

of a, as in late, ask, ball, hat, what.

of e, in meet, met.

of i, in find, pit.

of o, in note, not, move.

of u, in truth, but, bush.

of y, in try, pity.

The vowels have a long and a short sound, or quantity; and the different quantities are represented by different letters. Thus –

Long

a, in late,

ee, in feet,

oo, in pool,

a, in hall,

when shortened, is expressed

by e, as in let.

by i, in fit, & y in pity.

by u, in pull & oo in wool.

by o, in holly & a in wallow.

That the sounds of a in late and e in let are only a modification of the same vowel, may be easily understood by attending to the manner of forming the sounds; for in both words, the aperture of the mouth and the configuration of the organs are the same. The circumstance proves the sameness of the sound or vowel, in the two words, though differing in time or quantity.

A consonant is a letter which has no sound, or an imperfect one, without the help of a vowel. The consonants which are entirely silent, interrupt the voice by closing the organs; as b, d, g hard, k, p, t, which are called mutes; as in eb, ed, eg, ek, ep, et.

The consonants which do not entirely interrupt all sound by closing the organs, are f, l, m, n, r, s, v, z, which are all half vowels or semi-vowels – To these may be added the sounds of sh, th, zh, and ng, in esh, eth, ezh, ing, which our language has no single characters to express.

A dipthong is the union of two simple sounds uttered in one breath or articulation. The two sounds do not strictly form one; for there are two different positions of the organs, and two distinct sounds; but the transition from one to the other is so rapid that the distinction is scarcely perceived, and the sound is therefore considered as compound. Diphthongal sounds are sometimes represented by two letters, as in voice, joy, and sometimes by one, as in defy; the sound of y, in the latter word, if prolonged, terminates in e, and is really diphthongal.

A triphthong is a union of three vowels in a syllable; but it may be questioned whether in any English word, we pronounce three vowels in a single articulation. In the word adieu, the three vowels are not distinctly sounded.

B has but one sound, as in bite.

C is always sounded like k or s – like k, before a, o and u – and like s before e, i and y. Thus –

ca, ce, ci, co, cu, cy,

ka, se, si, ko, ku, sy.

At the end of words it is always hard like k, as in public. When followed by i or e before a vowel, the syllable slides into the sound of sh; as in cetaceous, gracious, social, which are pronounced cetashus, grashus, soshal.

D has only one sound, as in dress, bold.

F has its own proper sound, as in life, fever, except in of, where it has the sound of v.

G before a, o, and u has always its hard sound, as in gave, go, gun.

Before e, i, and y it has the same hard sound in some words, and in others, the sound of j. But these varieties are incapable of being reduced to any general rule, and are to be learned only by practice, observation, and a dictionary, in which the sounds are designated.

H can hardly be said to have any sound, but it denotes an aspiration or impulse of breath, which modifies the sound of the following vowel, as in heart, heave.

I is a vowel, as in fit; or a consonant as in bullion.

J is the mark of a compound sound, or union of sounds, which may be represented by dzh, or the soft g, as in jelly.

K has but one sound, as in king; and before n is always silent, as in know.

L has but one sound, as in lame. It is silent before k, as in walk.

M has but one sound, as in man; and is never silent.

N has but one sound, as in not, and is silent after m as in hymn.

P has one uniform sound, as in pit.

Q has the power of k, and is always followed by u, as in question.

R has one sound only, as in barrel.

S has the sound of c, as in so; of z as in rose; and where followed by i preceding a vowel, the syllable has the sound of sh, as in mission; or zh, as in osier.

T has its proper sound, as in turn, at the beginning of words and end of syllables. In all terminations in tion, and tial, ti have the sound of sh, as in nation, nuptial; except when preceded by s or x, in which cases they have the sound of ch, as in question.

U has the properties of a consonant and vowel, in union, unanimity, &c.

V has uniformly one sound, as in voice, live, and is never silent.

W has the power of a vowel, as in dwell, or a consonant, as in well, will.

X has the sound of ks, as in wax; or of gz, as in exist, and in other words, when followed by an accented syllable beginning with a vowel. In the beginning of Greek names, it has the sound of z, as in Xerxes, Xenophon.

Y is a vowel, as in vanity; a diphthong, as in defy; or a consonant, as in young.

Z has its own sound usually, as in zeal, freeze.

Ch have the sound of tsh in words of English origin, as in chip; in some words of French original, they have the sound of sh, as in machine; and some words of Greek origin, the sound of k, as in chorus.

Gh have the sound of f, as in laugh, or are silent, as in light.

Ph have the sound of f, as in Philosophy; except in Stephen, where the sound is that of v.

Ng have a nasal sound, as in sing; but when e follows ng, the latter takes the sound of j, as in range. In the words, longer, stronger, younger, the sound of the g is doubled, and the last syllable is sounded as if written long-ger, &c.

Sh has one sound only, as in shell; but its use is often supplied by ti, ci, and ce, before a vowel, as in motion, gracious, cetaceous.

Th has two sounds, aspirate and vocal – aspirate, as in think, bath; vocal, as in those, that, bathe.

Sc before a, o, u and r, are pronounced like sk, as in scale, scoff, sculpture, scribble: before e, i, y, like soft c, or s, as in scene, scent, science, Scythian. Thus pronounced,

sca, sce, sci, sco, scu, scy.

ska, se, si, sko, sku, sy.

Formation of Words and Sentences.

Letters form syllables, syllables form words, and words form sentences, which compose a discourse.

A syllable is a letter or a union of letters, which can be uttered at one impulse of voice.

A word of one syllable is called a monosyllable.

of two syllables	a dissyllable.
of three syllables	a trissyllable.
of many syllables	a polysyllable.

Of Accent, Emphasis, and Cadence.

Accent is a forcible stress or impulse of voice on a letter or syllable, distinguishing it from others in the same word. When it falls on a vowel, it prolongs the sound as in glory; when it falls on a consonant, the preceding vowel is short, as in habit.

The general rule by which accent is regulated, is that the stress of voice falls on that syllable of a word, which renders the articulation most easy to the speaker, and most agreeable to the hearer. By this rule has the accent of most words been imperceptibly established by long and universal consent.

When a word consists of three or more syllables, the ease of speaking requires usually a secondary accent, of less forcible utterance than the primary, but clearly distinguishable from the pronunciation of unaccented syllables; as superfluity, literary.

In many compound words, the parts of which are important words of themselves, there is very little distinction of accent, as ink-stand, church-yard.

Emphasis is a particular force of utterance given to a particular word in a sentence, on account of its importance.

Cadence is a fall or modulation of the voice in reading or speaking, especially at the end of a sentence.

Words are simple or compound, primitive or derivative.

A simple word cannot be divided without destroying the sense; as man, child, house, charity, faith.

A compound word is formed by two or more words; as chimney-piece, book-binder.

Primitive words are such as are not derived, but constitute a radical stock from which others are formed; as grace, hope, charm.

Derivative words are those which are formed of a primitive, and some termination or additional syllable; as grace-less, hope-ful, charm-ing, un-welcome.

Spelling is the art or practice of writing or reading the proper letters of a word; called also orthography. In forming tables for learners, the best rule to be observed, is to divide the syllables in such a manner as to guide the learner by the sound of the letters, to the sound of the words; that is, to divide them as they are divided in a just pronunciation.

Key to the following Work.

Long.		
1	1	1
a	name,	late.
e or ee	here,	feet.
i	time,	find.
o	note,	fort.
u or ew	tune,	new.
y	dry,	defy

Short.		
2	2	2
a	man,	hat.
e	men,	let.
i	pit,	pin.
u	tun,	but.
y	glory,	Egypt.

Broad a or aw.		
3	3	3
a	bald,	tall.
o	cost,	sought.
aw	law	

Flat a		
4	4	4
a	ask,	part.

Short aw.		
5	5	5
a	what,	was.
o	not,	from.

Oo proper.		
6	6	6
o or oo	move,	room.

Oo Short.		
7	7	7
oo	book,	stood.
u	bush,	full.

Short u.		
8	8	8
i	sir,	bird.
o	come,	love.
e	her.	

Long a.		
9	9	9
e	there,	vein.

Long e.		
10	10	10
i	fatigue,	pique.

oi, oy diphthong; voice, joy.
ou, ow diphthong; loud, now.

*This is not a letter, but a character standing for and. Children should therefore be taught to call it and; not and per se.

*They should be taught to pronounce ce, ci, cy, like se, si, sy.

EXPLANATION OF THE KEY.

A figure stands as the invariable representative of a certain sound. The figure 1 represents the long sound of the letters, a, e, i, o, u, or ew, and y; number 2, the short sound of the same characters; number 3 marks the sound of broad a, as in hall; number 4 represents the sound of a, in father; number 5 represents the short sound of broad a, as in not, what; number 6 represents the sound of o in move, commonly expressed oo; number 7 represents the short sound of oo in root, bush; number 8 represents the sound of u short, made by e, i, and o, as in her, bird, come, pronounced hur, burd, cum; number 9 represents the first sound of a made by e, as in their, vein, pronounced thare, vane; number 10 represents the French sound of i, which is the same as e long.

The sounds of the diphthongs oi and ou are not represented by figures; these have one invariable sound, and are placed before the words where they occur in the tables.

Silent letters are printed in Italic characters. Thus in head, goal, build, people, fight, the Italic letters have no sound.

S, when printed in Italic, is not silent, but pronounced like z, as in devise, pronounced devize.

The letter e at the end of words of more syllables than one, is almost always silent: but serves often to lengthen a foregoing vowel, as in bid, bide; to soften c, as in notice; or to soften g, as in homage; or to change the sound of th from the first to the second, as in bath, bathe. In the following work, when e final lengthens the foregoing vowel, that is, gives it its first sound, it is printed in a Roman character, as in fate; but in all other cases it is printed in Italic, except in table 39.

Ch have the English sound, as in charm; except in the 38th and 39th tables.

The sounds of th in this and thou, are all distinguished in the 12th and 37th tables; except in numeral adjectives.

The sound of aw is invariably that of broad a; and that of ew nearly the same as u long.

N. B. Although one character is sufficient to express a simple sound, yet the combinations ee, aw, ew, oo, are so well known to express certain sounds, that it was judged best to print both letters in Roman characters. Ck and ss are also printed in Roman characters, though one, alone would be sufficient to express the sound.

THE ALPHABET.

Roman Letters.	Italic.	Names of Letters.
a A	*a A*	a
b B	*b B*	be
c C	*c C*	ce
d D	*d D*	de
e E	*e E*	e
f F	*f F*	ef
g G	*g G*	je
h H	*h H*	he, or avtch
i I	*i I*	i
j J	*j J*	ja
k K	*k K*	ka
l L	*l L*	el
m M	*m M*	em
n N	*n N*	en
o O	*o O*	o
p P	*p P*	pe
q Q	*q Q*	cu
r R	*r R*	er
s S	*s S*	es
t T	*t T*	te
u U	*u U*	u
v V	*v V*	ve
w W	*w W*	oo
x X	*x X*	eks
y Y	*y Y*	wi or ye
z Z	*z Z*	ze
&*	*&**	and

Double LETTERS

ff, ffl, fi, fl, ffi, fh.

TABLE I

LESSON I.
ba be bi bo bu by
ca ce* ci* co cu cy*
da de di do du dy
fa fe fi fo fu fy
ka ke ki ko ku ky

LESSON II.
ga ge gi go gu gy
ha he hi ho hu hy
ma me mi mo mu my
na ne ni no nu ny
ra re ri ro ru ry
ta te ti to tu ty
wa we wi wo wu wy

LESSON III.
la le li lo lu ly
pa pe pi po pu py
sa se si so su sy
za ze zi zo zu zy

LESSON IV.
ab eb ib ob ub
ac ec ic oc uc
ad ed id od ud
af ef if of uf
al el il ol ul

LESSON V.
ag eg ig og ug
am em im om um
an en in on un
ap ep ip op up
as es is os us
av ev iv ov uv
ax ex ix ox ux

LESSON VI.
ak ek ik ok uk
at et it ot ut
ar er ir or ur
az ez iz oz uz

LESSON VII.
bla ble bli blo blu
cla cle cli clo clu
pla ple pli plo plu
fla fle fli flo flu
va ve vi vo vu

LESSON VIII.
bra bre bri bro bru
cra cre cri cro cru
pra pre pri pro pru
gra gre gri gro gru
pha phe phi pho phu

LESSON IX.
cha che chi cho chu chy
dra dre dri dro dru dry
fra fre fri fro fru fry
gla gle gli glo glu gly

LESSON X.
sla sle sli slo slu sly
qua que qui quo
sha she shi sho shu shy
spa spe spi spo spu spy

LESSON XI.
sta ste sti sto stu sty
sca sce sci sco scu scy
tha the thi tho thu thy
tra tre tri tro tru try

* They should be taught to pronounce them ce, ci cy, lik se, si, sy.

LESSON XII.

spla	sple	spli	splo	splu	sply
spra	spre	spri	spro	spru	spry
stra	stre	stri	stro	stru	stry
swa	swe	swi	swo	swu	swy

TABLE II.

Words of one syllable.

Note: A figure placed over the first word marks the sound of the vowel in all that follow in that column, until contradicted by another figure.

LESSON I.

ba^{2}g	bi^{5}g	bo^{2}g	bu^{2}g	de^{2}n	ca^{2}p	bi^{2}t	do^{5}t
fag	dig	dog	dug	hen	gap	fit	got
lag	fig	fog	hug	men	lap	hit	hot
gag	gig	hog	lug	pen	map	pit	jot
hag	pig	jog	mug	ten	rap	sit	lot
rag	wig	log	tug	wen	tap	wit	not

LESSON II.

ma^{2}n	fo^{5}b	ba^{2}d	be^{2}d	bi^{2}d	fo^{5}p	be^{2}t	bu^{2}t
can	job	had	fed	did	hop	get	cut
pan	mob	lad	led	lid	lop	let	hut
ran	rob	mad	red	hid	mop	met	nut
van	sob	sad	wed	rid	top	yet	rut

LESSON III

be^{2}lt	gi^{2}lt	ba^{2}nd	ble^{2}d	bra^{2}g	clo^{5}d	bra^{2}d
melt	hilt	hand	bred	drag	plod	clad
felt	milt	land	fled	flag	shod	glad
pelt	jilt	sand	shed	stag	trod	shad

LESSON IV.

clo^{5}g	glu^{2}t	bla^{2}b	chu^{2}b	da^{2}mp	bu^{2}mp	be^{2}nd
flog	shut	drab	club	camp	jump	lend
frog	smut	crab	drub	lamp	lump	mend
grog	slut	scab	grub	vamp	pump	send

LESSON V.

bi^{1}nd	bo^{1}ld	ca^{3}ll	bi^{2}ll	be^{2}nt	be^{2}st	bri^{2}m
find	hold	fall	fill	dent	lest	grim
mind	fold	gall	hill	lent	nest	skim
kind	sold	hall	kill	sent	jest	swim
wind	gold	tall	mill	went	pest	trim

LESSON VI.

la^{1}ce	di^{1}ce	fa^{1}de	bi^{1}de	ca^{1}ge	ba^{1}ke	di^{1}ne
mace	mice	lade	ride	page	cake	fine
trace	nice	made	side	rage	make	pine
pace	rice	wade	wide	wage	wake	wine

LESSON VII.

ga^{1}le	ca^{1}pe	pi^{1}pe	co^{1}pe	di^{1}re	da^{1}te	dri^{1}ve
pale	rape	ripe	hope	hire	hate	five
sale	tape	wipe	rope	fire	fate	hive
vale	ape	type	pope	wire	grate	rive

LESSON VIII.

dote	file	dame	fare	bore	bone	nose
mote	bile	fame	mare	fore	cone	dose
note	pile	came	rare	tore	hone	hose
vote	vile	name	tare	wore	tone	rose

TABLE III.

LESSON I.

bla^{2}nk	blu^{2}sh	fle^{1}et	bra^{1}ce	pri^{1}ce	bri^{1}ne
flank	flush	sheet	trace	slice	shine
frank	plush	street	grace	spice	swine
prank	crush	greet	space	twice	twine

LESSON II.

ba^{2}nd	ble^{2}ss	cri^{1}me	bro^{1}ke	bla^{1}de	bla^{1}me
grand	dress	chime	choke	spade	flame
stand	press	prime	stoke	trade	shame
strand	stress	slime	smoke	shade	frame

LESSON III.

bra^{1}ke	gla^{1}re	bra^{1}ve	he^{2}nce	mi^{2}nce	ble^{1}ed
drake	share	crave	fence	since	breed
flake	snare	grave	pence	prince	speed
spake	spare	slave	sense	rinse	steed

LESSON IV.

and	i^{2}ll	a^{1}ge	hi^{2}s	ri^{2}ch	le^{2}ss	du^{1}ke	li^{1}fe
act	ink	aim	has	held	mess	mule	wife
apt	fact	aid	hast	gift	kiss	rule	safe
ell	fan	ice	hath	dull	miss	time	male
ebb	left	ale	add	till	mush	tune	save
egg	self	ace	elf	will	hush	mute	here
end	else	ape	pen	well	desk	maze	robe

LESSON V.

gla^{1}de	snake	tra^{2}ct	cla^{2}nk	cla^{2}mp	bla^{2}ck
grade	glaze	pact	crank	champ	crack
shave	craze	plant	shank	cramp	match
wave	prate	sang	plank	spasm	patch
quake	slate	fang	clump	splash	fetch
sta^{1}ge	shape	rang	thump	crash	vetch

LESSON VI.

mi^{1}ne	si^{1}re	stri^{1}fe	bri^{1}de	bri^{2}ck	stri^{1}ve
spine	quire	fife	chide	kick	spike
vine	spire	trite	glide	chick	splice
gripe	mire	quite	pride	click	strike
snipe	smite	squire	vice	lick	ride
stripe	spite	spike	trice	stick	wide

LESSON VII.

Examples of the formation of the plural from the singular, and of other derivatives.

name, names	camp, camps	slave, slaves
dame, dames	clamp, clamps	brave, braves
gale, gales	lamp, lamps	stave, staves
scale, scales	scalp, scalps	mate, mates
cape, capes	map, maps	state, states
grape, grapes	plant, plants	mind, minds
crane, cranes	plank, planks	bind, binds
shade, shades	flag, flags	snare, snares
grade, grades	bank, banks	snake, snakes

LESSON VIII.

cake, cakes	street, streets	club, clubs
flake, flakes	sheet, sheets	vote, votes
hope, hopes	chap, chaps	cone, cones
note, notes	flank, flanks	bone, bones
blot, blots	shine, shines	shake, shakes
cube, cubes	slope, slopes	spade, spades
grave, graves	fold, folds	pipe, pipes

wire, wires	pine, pines	mill, mills
hive, hives	fade, fades	hill, hills

LESSON IX.

side, sides	blank, blanks	mare, mares
vale, vales	choke, chokes	tare, tares
wife, wives	stoke, stokes	grate, grates
life, lives	smoke, smokes	smite, smites
hive, hives	flame, flames	brick, bricks
drive, drives	frame, frames	kick, kicks
go, goes	stand, stands	stick, sticks
woe, woes	drove, droves	bride, brides
do, does	robe, robes	fire, fires
add, adds	spot, spots	smell, smells
lad, lads	flag, flags	swim, swims

TABLE IV.

Easy words of two syllables, accented on the first.

When the stress of voice falls on a vowel, it is necessarily long, and is marked by the figure 1. When the stress of voice falls on a consonant, the preceding vowel is necessarily short, and is marked by figure 2.

No figures are placed over the vowels in unaccented syllables, because they are short. It must be observed, however, that in unaccented terminating syllables, almost all vowels are pronounced like i and u short. Thus,

al is pronounced ul, rural rurul,

et   it, fillet fillit.

This is the general rule in the language; originating doubtless from this cause, that short i and u are pronounced with a less aperture or opening of the mouth, with less exertions of the organs, and consequently with more ease than the other vowels in these terminating syllables; for in order to pronounce them right, nothing more is requisite than to lay a proper stress of the voice on the accented syllable, and pronounce the unaccented syllables with more ease and rapidity. When any of these terminations are accented, as some of them are, the vowel retains its own sound; as, compel, lament, depress, &c.

The figures are placed next to the vowels of the accented syllables; and one figure marks all the words that follow, till it is contradicted by another figure.

ba¹ ker	li on	to ry	chap man
pri er	ma ker	to tal	chap ter
ci der	mo dish	tri al	chat ter
cra zy	mo ment	tru ant	child ren
cri er	o ver	tu mult	chil ly
cru el	pa gan	tu tor	cin der
di al	pa per	va cant	cut ler
di et	pa pist	va grant	dan ger
du ty	pi lot	va ry	dif fer
dy er	pli ant	vi per	din ner
dra per	po et	vi tal	drum mer
fa tal	pre cept	vo cal	el der
fe ver	pru dent	wa fer	em bers
fi nal	qui et	wa ges	em blem
fla grant	ra ker	wa ger	en ter
flu ent	re al	woe ful	fac tor
fo cus	ri der	a²b bot	fag got
fru gal	ri ot	act or	fan cy
fu el	ru by	ad der	fat ling
glo ry	ru in	ad vent	fer ret
gi ant	ru ler	al um	fil let
gra vy	ru ral	am ber	flan nel
gru el	sa cred	an gel	flat ter
ho ly	se cret	bal lad	flut ter
hu man	sha dy	bank er	fran tic
i cy	si lent	ban ter	fun nel
i dol	so ber	bap tist	gal lop
i vy	spi der	bat ter	gam mon
ju ry	sto ry	bet ter	gan der
ju lep	stu dent	bit ter	gar ret
la dy	stu pid	blun der	gen try
la zy	ta per	buf fet	gib bet
le gal	tra der	car rot	gip sy
li ar	ti dings	chan nel	glim mer

glit ter	nurs ling	splen did	cho⁵p per
gul let	pam per	splen dor	com ment
gun ner	pan el	splin ter	com mon
gus set	pan try	stam mer	con duct
gut ter	pat tern	sub ject	con cord
ham let	pat ron	sud den	con gress
hap py	pen cil	suf fer	con quest
hin der	pen ny	sul len	con sul
hun dred	pep per	sul try	con vert
hunt er	pil lar	sum mon	doc tor
in sect	pil fer	tal ly	dross y
in step	pil grim	tan ner	dol lar
in to	plum met	tat tler	fod der
jest er	pup py	tem per	fol ly
ken nel	ran som	ten der	fop pish
kind red	rec tor	ten dril	hor rid
king dom	rem nant	ten ter	joc ky
kins man	ren der	tim ber	jol ly
lad der	ren net	trench er	mot to
lan tern	rub bish	trump et	on set
lap pet	sal ad	tum bler	of fer
lat ter	sand y	tur key	of fice
let ter	sat in	vel lum	pot ter
lim ber	scan dal	vel vet	rob ber
lit ter	scat ter	ves sel	sot tish
luck y	sel dom	vic tim	cle²r gy
mam mon	self ish	vul gar	er rand
man na	sen tence	ug ly	her mit
man ner	shat ter	ul cer	ker nel
mat ron	shep herd	un der	mer cy
mem ber	shil ling	up per	per fect
mer ry	sig nal	ut most	per son
mill er	sil ver	ut ter	ser mon
mit ten	sin ner	wed ding	ser pent
mur der	slat tern	wil ful	serv ant
mud dy	slen der	will ing	ver min
mur mur	slum ber	wis dom	ven om
mut ter	smug gler	a⁴rt less	
num ber	spin net	art ist	
nut meg	spir it	af ter	

TABLE V.

Easy words of two syllables, accented on the second.

N. B. In general, when a vowel in an unaccented syllable stands alone or ends a syllable, it has its first sound, as in protect; yet we do not dwell upon the vowel; it is short and weak. When the vowel, in such syllables, is joined to a consonant, it has its second sound, as address.

* But if a vowel unaccented ends the word, it has its second sound, as in city.

a ba¹se	dis place	pre pare	ad dress
a bide	dis robe	pro mote	ad mit
a dore	dis taste	re bate	a mend
a like	di vine	re buke	a midst
al lude	e lope	re cite	ar range
a lone	en dure	re cline	as cend
a maze	en force	re duce	be set
as pire	en gage	re late	ca nal
at one	en rage	re ly	col lect
at tire	en roll	re mind	com pel
be fore	en sue	re plete	con duct
be have	en tice	re vere	con tend
be hold	en tire	se duce	con tent
com ply	e vade	sub lime	cor rect
com pute	for sworn	su pine	cor rupt
com plete	fore seen	su preme	de duct
con fine	im brue	sur vive	de fect
con jure	im pale	tra duce	de fend
con sume	in cite	trans late	de press
con trol	in flame	un bind	de range
cre ate	in trude	un told	de tect
de cide	in sure	un fold	di rect
de clare	in vite	un glue	dis band
de duce	mis name	un kind	dis miss
de fy	mis place	un lace	dis sent
de fine	mis rule	un ripe	dis tinct
de grade	mis take	un safe	dis trust
de note	mo rose	ab ru²pt	dis tract
de pute	par take	ab surd	dis turb
de rive	per spire	ac cept	ef fect
dis like	po lite	ad dict	e mit

en camp	mis trust	ro mance	en chant
en rich	mo lest	se dan	en large
e vent	neg lect	se lect	huz za
e vince	ob struct	sub ject	un arm
ful fil	oc cur	sub mit	un bar
fi nance	of fence	sub tract	ab ho⁵r
gal lant	o mit	sus pense	re volve
him self	op press	trans act	re volt
im pend	per mit	trans cend	de spond
im plant	por tend	trans gress	un lock
im press	pre tend	trans plant	con ce²rt
im print	pre dict	tre pan	de fer
in apt	pro ject	un bend	di vert
in cur	pro tect	un fit	in verse
in dent	pro test	un hinge	in vert
in fect	re cant	un hurt	per vert
in fest	re fit	un man	per verse
in flict	re lax	de ba⁴r	re fer
in still	re mit	de part	con fer
in struct	re press	dis arm	de ter
in vest	re tract	dis card	in fer
mis give	re trench	em balm	in ter
mis print	ro bust	em bark	in tend

TABLE VI.

Easy words of three syllables; the full accent on the first, and a weak accent on the third.

cru¹ ci fix	li bra ry	se cre cy	ac cid ent
cru el ty	lu na cy	scru ti ny	al im ent
de cen cy	no ta ry	si mon y	ad a mant
di a dem	nu mer al	stu pi fy	am i ty
di a lect	nu trim ent	tu te lar	am nes ty
dra per y	o ver plus	va can cy	ar ro gant
droll e ry	po et ry	va gran cy	bar ris ter
du ti ful	pri ma cy	a²b do men	but ter y
flu en cy	pri ma ry	al le gro	ben e fit
i ro ny	pu ri ty	ad mi ral	big a my
i vo ry	re gen cy	an im al	big ot ry
la zi ness	ru dim ent	an nu al	but ter fly

cal i co	fam i ly	med ic al	sen a tor
cal en dar	fel o ny	mel o dy	sen ti ment
cab in et	fes tiv al	mem o ry	sen tin el
can is ter	fin ic al	mes sen ger	sev er al
can ni bal	fish er y	mil lin er	syl la bub
can o py	gal lant ry	min er al	sim il ar
cap i tal	gal le ry	min is ter	sin gu lar
chast i ty	gar ri son	mus cu lar	sin is ter
cin na mon	gen e ral	mys te ry	slip pe ry
cit i zen	gun ner y	nat u ral	sub si dy
clar i fy	hap pi ness	pan o ply	sum ma ry
clas sic al	her ald ry	par a dox	sup ple ment
clem en cy	im ple ment	par a gon	sym me try
cler ic al	im pu dent	par al lax	tam a rind
cur ren cy	in cre ment	par al lel	tap es try
cyl in der	in di go	par a pet	tem po ral
den i zen	in dus try	par i ty	ten den cy
det rim ent	in fan cy	pat ri ot	ten e ment
dif fid ent	in fant ry	ped ant ry	ter ri fy
dif fer ent	in fi del	ped i gree	tes ta ment
dif fi cult	in stru ment	pen al ty	tit u lar
dig ni ty	in te ger	pen u ry	typ ic al
dil i gent	in tel lect	pes ti lent	tyr an ny
div id end	in ter est	pil lo ry	vag a bond
dul cim er	in ter val	prac tic al	van i ty
ec sta cy	in va lid	prin cip al	vic tor y
ed it or	jus ti fy	pub lic an	vil la ny
ef fe gy	leg a cy	punc tu al	vin e gar
el em ent	len i ty	pun gen cy	ur gen cy
el e gy	lep ro sy	pyr a mid	wag gon er
em bas sy	lev i ty	rad ic al	wil der ness
eb o ny	lib er al	rar i ty	har[2] bin ger
em bry o	lib er ty	reg u lar	har mo ny
em e rald	lig a ment	rem e dy	harp si chord
em pe ror	lin e al	rib ald ry	cod[5] i cil
en e my	lit a ny	rev er end	col o ny
en mi ty	lit er al	rit u al	com e dy
en ti ty	lit ur gy	riv u let	com ic al
ep i gram	lux u ry	sac ra ment	con ju gal
es cu lent	man i fest	sal a ry	con tin ent
ev e ry	man i fold	sat is fy	con tra band
fac ul ty	man ner ly	sec u lar	con tra ry
fac tor y	mar in er	sed im ent	doc u ment

drop sic al
glob u lar
gloss a ry
hos pi tal
lot te ry
mon u ment
nom in al
oc u lar
oc cu py
of fi cer

or a tor
or i gin
or na ment
or re ry
ot to man
pol i cy
pol i tic
pop u lar
pov er ty
pon der ous

prob i ty
prod i gal
prod i gy
prom in ent
prop er ty
pros o dy
prot est ant
quad ru ped
qual i ty
quan ti ty

quan da ry
cer² ti fy
mer cu ry
per fi dy
per ju ry
per ma nent
per tin ent
reg u late
ter ma gant

TABLE VII.

Easy words of three syllables, accented on the second.

a ba¹se ment
a gree ment
al li ance
al lure ment
ap pa rent
ar ri val
a maze ment
at one ment
co e qual
con fine ment
con trol ler
de ci pher
de co rum
de ni al
de cri al
de port ment
de po nent
dic ta tor
di plo ma
en roll ment
en tice ment
e qua tor
he ro ic
il le gal
im pru dent
oc ta vo
op po nent

po ma tum
pri me val
re ci tal
re li ance
re qui tal
re vi val
spec ta tor
sub scri ber
sur vi vor
tes ta tor
tes ta trix
trans la tor
trans pa rent
tri bu nal
ver ba tim
vol ca no
un e qual
un mind ful
a ba²n don
ac cus tom
af fect ed
ag gress or
a mend ment
ap par el
ap pend ix
as cend ant
as sas sin

as sem bly
at tach ment
at tend ant
be gin ning
be wil der
co hab it
col lect or
con sid er
con tin gent
con tract or
de cant er
de lin quent
de liv er
de mer it
de tach ment
di lem ma
di min ish
dis sent er
dis tem per
dis tin guish
di ur nal
dog mat ic
do mes tic
dra mat ic
e ject ment
em bar rass
em bel lish

em pan el
en camp ment
e quip ment
er rat ic
es tab lish
hys ter ic
in ces sant
in clem ent
in cum bent
in hab it
in sip id
in trin sic
in val id
ma lig nant
mo nas tic
noc tur nal
pa cif ic
pe dant ic
po lem ic

pre cept or
pre tend er
pro hib it
pro lif ic
pro tect or
pu is sant
re dund ant
re fresh ment
re lin quish
re luct ant
re mem ber
re plen ish
re plev in
re pug nant
re pub lish
ro man tic
se ques ter
spe cif ic
sur ren der

to bac co
trans cend ent
trans gress or
tri umph ant
um brel la
a bo⁵l ish
ac com plish
ad mon ish
as ton ish
de mol ish
dis solv ent
im mod est
im mor tal
im pos tor
im prop er
in con stant
in sol vent
im mor al
un god ly

TABLE VIII.

Easy words of three syllables, accented on the first and third.

al a mo¹de
dev o tee
dis a gree
dis es teem
dom i neer
im ma ture
im por tune
in com mode
in ter cede
in tro duce
mis ap ply
mis be have

o ver take
rec on cile
ref u gee
su per sede
su per scribe
vol un teer
un der mine
ap pre he²nd
con de scend
con tra dict
dis pos sess
in di rect

in cor rect
in ter mix
o ver run
o ver turn
rec ol lect
rec om mend
rep re hend
su per add
un der stand
un der sell
dis con cern
dis con nect

TABLE IX.

Easy words of four syllables, the full accent on the first, and the half accent on the third.

lu¹ mi na ry	in ti ma cy	sump tu a ry
mo ment a ry	in tri ca cy	ter ri to ry
nu ga to ry	in vent o ry	tes ti mo ny
bre vi a ry	man da to ry	trib u ta ry
a²c cu ra cy	mat ri mo ny	per emp to ry
ac cri mo ny	mer ce na ry	sub lu na ry
ad mi ral ty	mis cel la ny	co⁵n tro ver sy
ad ver sa ry	mil i ta ry	mon as te ry
al i mo ny	pat ri mo ny	ob sti na cy
al le go ry	plan et a ry	prom is so ry
cer e mo ny	preb end a ry	prom on to ry
cus tom a ry	pref a to ry	vol un ta ry
del i ca cy	pur ga to ry	ob du ra cy
dif fi cult y	sal u ta ry	com ment a ry
dil a to ry	sanc tu a ry	con tu ma cy
ep i lep sy	sec re ta ry	con tu me ly
em is sa ry	sed en ta ry	drom e da ry
ig no min y	stat u a ry	com mis sa ry

The words het-e-ro-dox, lin-e-a-ment, pat-ri-ot-ism, sep-tu-a-gint, have the full accent on the first syllable, and the half accent on the last.

TABLE X.

Easy words of four syllables accented on the second.

a e¹ ri al	cor po re al	ma te ri al
an nu i ty	cre du li ty	ma tu ri ty
ar mo ri al	cri te ri on	me mo ri al
cen tu ri on	e le gi ac	mer cu ri al
col le gi al	fu tu ri ty	out rage ous ly
com mu ni cant	gram ma ri an	ob scu ri ty
com mu ni ty	gra tu i ty	ob tain a ble
con gru i ty	his to ri an	pro pri e ty
con nu bi al	li bra ri an	se cu ri ty

so bri e ty
va cu i ty
va ri e ty
ab su²rd i ty
ac tiv i ty
ac cess a ry
ac cess o ry
ad min is ter
ad vers i ty
a dul te ry
af fin i ty
a nal o gy
a nat o my
an tag o nist
ar til le ry
a vid i ty
bar bar i ty
bru tal i ty
ca lam i ty
cap tiv i ty
ce lib a cy
ci vil i ty
cli mac ter ic
co in ci dent
col lat e ral
com par i son
com pet it or
com pul so ry
con jec tur al
con spir a cy
con stit u ent
de cliv i ty
de lin quen cy
de prav i ty
di am e ter
dis par i ty
di vin i ty
ef fect u al
e lec tric al
em py re al
e pis co pal
e pit o me
e quiv a lent

e quiv o cal
e van gel ist
e vent u al
fa tal i ty
fer til i ty
fes tiv i ty
fi del i ty
for mal i ty
fru gal i ty
gram mat i cal
ha bit u al
hos til i ty
hu man i ty
hu mil i ty
i den ti ty
im mens i ty
im ped i ment
ju rid i cal
le vit i cal
lon gev i ty
ma lev o lent
ma lig ni ty
mil len ni um
mo ral i ty
mu nif i cent
na tiv i ty
ne ces si ty
no bil i ty
nu mer i cal
om nip o tent
par tic u lar
per pet u al
po lit i cal
po lyg a my
pos ter i ty
pre cip i tant
pre dic a ment
pro fund i ty
pros per i ty
ra pid i ty
re cip ro cal
re pub li can
sab bat i cal

sa tan i cal
scur ril i ty
se ver i ty
sig nif i cant
se ren i ty
sin cer i ty
so lem ni ty
su prem a cy
ter res tri al
tran quil li ty
ty ran ni cal
va lid i ty
ve nal i ty
vi cin i ty
a po⁵l o gy
a pos ta cy
as trol o gy
as tron o my
bi og ra phy
com mod i ty
con com i tant
de moc ra cy
de spond en cy
e con o my
ge om e try
hy poc ri sy
ma jor i ty
me trop o lis
mi nor i ty
mo nop o ly
pre dom i nate
pri or i ty
tau tol o gy
ver bos i ty
ad ve²r si ty
di ver si ty
e ter ni ty
hy per bo le
pro verb i al
sub serv i ent

TABLE XI.

Easy words of four syllables; the full accent on the third, and the half accent on the first.

an te ce¹ dent	man i fest o
ap par ra tus	at mos pher ic
com ment a tor	mem o ran dum
me di a tor	o ri en tal
sa cer do tal	or na men tal
su per vi sor	pan e gy ric
ac ci de²nt al	pre de ces sor
ar o mat ic	sci en tif ic
cal i man co	sys tem at ic
det ri men tal	cor res po⁵n dent
en er get ic	hor i zon tal
fun da men tal	u ni ve²r sal
in nu en do	un der stand ing
mal e fac tor	o ver whelm ing

Having proceeded through tables, composed of easy words from one to four syllables, let the learner begin the following tables, which consist of more difficult words. In these the child will be much assisted by a knowledge of the figures and the use of the Italics.

If the instructor should think it useful to let his pupils read some of the easy lessons before they have finished spelling, he may divide their studies – let them spell one part of the day, and read the other.

TABLE XII.

Difficult and irregular Monosyllables.

I would recommend this table to be read sometimes across the page.

ba¹y	pay	ray	pail	nail
day	pray	bray	sail	trail
hay	sway	stray	rail	bail
lay	fray	slay	frail	ail
say	clay	spay	wail	hail
may	way	jail	mail	tail

flail	vain	date	key	steer
snail	wain	tale	leap	bier
laird	paint	staid	neap	tier
aid	quaint	laid	reap	year
maid	plaint	paid	cheap	creed
stair	aim	braid	heap	heed
swear	claim	air	steel	mead
wear	main	chair	kneel	knead
bear	waif	fair	squeal	reed
tear	stage	hair	beer	bleed
brain	gauge	pair	peer	breed
chain	plague	lain	deer	plead
grain	vague	change	fear	deem
slain	bait	strange	dear	seem
train	great	blaze	hear	cream
rain	gait	be	near	dream
main	tray	pea	rear	stream
plain	gay	sea	veer	beam
sprain	slay	tea	drear	steam
stain	play	flea	clear	seam
twain	beard	yea	shear	gleam
wait	drain	seal	weed	leaf
plait	fain	steal	bead	sheaf
strait	faint	veal	lead	fief
graze	taint	weal	read	lief
praise	saint	zeal	seed	beef
raise	trait	peal	scream	plea
daze	haste	real	fleam	flee
haze	paste	ceil	fream	bee
shave	waste	eel	ream	deep
grave	baste	cheer	team	keep
brave	chaste	heard	least	seep
knave	taste	blear	feast	weep
break	traipse	ear	yeast	steep
steak	teal	sear	beast	sleep
spray	feel	smear	priest	creep
tray	keel	spear	east	sheep
gray	deal	tear	reef	fleece
pain	heal	queer	grief	peace
strain	meal	deed	brief	cease
gain	peel	feed	chief	teat
plain	reel	need	deaf	beak

leak	beeves	sky	guile	bean
weak	eaves	lie	mild	clean
bleak	greaves	die	child	mien
sneak	freeze	eye	lease	queen
speak	sneeze	buy	geese	wean
freak	breeze	try	niece	keen
squeak	ease	fry	piece	glean
reek	squeeze	sleight	grease	spleen
cheek	cheese	bright	crease	dean
wreak	frieze	fight	meet	green
fleak	please	blight	bleat	quean
screak	league	fright	cheat	yean
shriek	teague	flight	treat	lean
sleek	tweag	wight	meat	mean
streak	leash	wright	seat	heave
sleeve	liege	clime	feat	cleave
grieve	siege	rhyme	beat	seize
reeve	dry	knife	neat	tease
leave	bye	climb	feet	speech
lieve	fly	smile	eat	leach
reave	cry	stile	seen	beach
reach	light	owe	coast	port
teach	might	flow	toast	fort
screech	height	glow	more	sport
breach	night	blow	four	court
bleach	right	slow	pour	goad
each	sight	know	door	load
peach	tight	grow	floor	toad
fiend	slight	snow	roar	woad
yield	wild	stow	boar	soap
shield	bride	strow	hoar	froze
wield	stride	dough	oar	hoarse
field	guide	hoe	soar	source
pie	guise	sloe	oat	coarse
wry	fro	mole	boat	board
high	doe	pole	doat	hoard
nigh	toe	sole	loan	gourd
sigh	foe	foal	shown	sword
by	bow	goal	old	holme
fie	mow	roll	told	oaf
hie	tow	poll	cold	loaf
vie	row	roast	mold	due

true	boll	float	broach	blew
you	toll	joke	folks	drew
glue	soul	oak	coax	knew
sue	scroll	croak	foam	crew
dew	coal	cloke	roam	hew
rue	shoal	soak	comb	strew
shrew	bowl	tone	loam	shew
spew	knoll	own	shorn	slew
stew	stroll	known	sworn	blue
tew	troll	groan	mourn	shrewd
yew	brogue	blown	force	crude
chew	rogue	flown	course	feud
clew	vogue	mown	few	rheum
ewe	most	sown	new	muse
slue	post	moan	pew	bruise
mew	host	close	lieu	use
cure	ghost	prose	view	cruise
pure	boast	chose	flew	spruce
your	goat	coach	grew	use
rude	moat	poach	screw	juice
prude	bloat	roach	brew	cruse
sluice	strap	guest	singe	much
fruit	check	sweat	cringe	such
bruit	speck	debt	fringe	wrap
suit	wreck	stem	twinge	shall
mewl	meant	phlegm	glimpse	bled
lure	sense	wink	since	dead
ja²mb	tense	pink	rinse	stead
lamb	bench	cinque	jolt	read
plaid	clench	prism	bolt	tread
limb	stench	schism	dolt	bread
gaunt	quench	chip	moult	dread
dense	wench	skip	coat	spread
hence	wrench	skill	dost	shred
pence	drench	spill	cu²rl	head
fence	fetch	chill	hurl	cleanse
lapse	sketch	ditch	churl	realm
flat	wretch	pitch	drum	dram
gnat	delve	witch	dumb	deck
cash	valve	twitch	crumb	neck
clash	guess	niche	numb	peck
gnash	breast	hinge	plum	spend

friend	chin	spit	lurch	taw
blend	twin	knit	church	maw
badge	skin	twit	young	raw
fadge	guilt	live	gulf	paw
edge	built	sieve	nymph	saw
hedge	quilt	ridge	hymn	awe
wedge	build	no¹ne	judge	gnaw
sledge	drift	stone	grudge	straw
ledge	shift	home	drudge	flaw
sedge	swift	bolt	trudge	draw
pledge	twist	colt	shrub	chaw
dredge	wrist	touch	scrub	claw
fledge	risk	crutch	bulge	craw
bridge	shrill	burst	gurge	haw
bilge	wince	stuff	surge	jaw
helve	teint	snuff	purge	cost*
twelve	brick	rough	plunge	lost
ship	stick	tough	curse	tost
strip	kick	plump	purse	war
scrip	wick	stump	la³w	for**
spin	quick	trump	shaw	nor**
taught	warn	lord	call	wart
caught	corse	ward	wall	sort
brought	horn	gauze	maul	short
sought	morn	cause	scrawl	quart
ought	fawn	pause	sprawl	snort
wrought	lawn	clause	squall	bald
fought	dawn	torch	yawl	scald
groat	pawn	scorch	awl	off
fraught	sawn	gorge	haul	oft
naught	brawn	all	stall	loft
form	spawn	tall	small	soft
storm	yawn	fall	crawl	cross
swarm	laud	hall	brawl	dross
warm	fraud	gall	bawl	moss
born	broad	pall	caul	loss
corn	cord	ball	drawl	horse

*Perhaps o and a in the words cost, born, warm, &c. may be considered as coming more properly under the figure 5. But the liquids that follow them have such an effect in lengthening the syllables, that it appears more natural to place them under figure 3. A similar remark applies to a in bar.

**These words, when unemphatical, are necessarily short.

corps*e*	pa*l*m	clasp	scarp	ha*l*f
dwarf	psa*l*m	hasp	carve	ca*l*f
co*u*gh	qua*l*m	rasp	starve	la*u*gh
tro*u*gh	a*l*ms	gasp	arm	craft
fork	bask	grasp	harm	shaft
cork	cask	hard	charm	waft
hawk	ask	bard	farm	raft
ba*l*k	mask	card	barm	dra*u*ght
wa*l*k	task	lard	art	aft
ta*l*k	ark	guard	cart	haft
cha*l*k	bark	pard	dart	pant
sta*l*k	dark	yard	hart	grant
ca*l*k	hark	branch	mart	slant
da*u*b	mark	lanch	part	ant
bawd	lark	staunch	tart	a*u*nt
warp	park	haunch	start	da*u*nt
wasp	spark	blanch	smart	fla*u*nt
want	arc	craunch	chart	ha*u*nt
sa*u*ce	shark	carp	h*ea*rt	ja*u*nt
ba⁴*l*m	stark	harp	staff	ta*u*nt
ca*l*m	asp	sharp	chaff	va*u*nt
cast	larg*e*	jar	drop	fond
past	barg*e*	mar	crop	pond
last	farc*e*	par	shop	wand
vast	pars*e*	barb	shock	strong
blast	ca*l*ve	garb	wan	*w*rong
fast	ha*l*ve	carl*e*	swan	botch
mast	sa*l*ve	marl	gon*e*	scotch
mass	gape	snarl	wash	mosq*ue*
pass	carn	chanc*e*	swash	blot
lass	darn	danc*e*	watch	ya*ch*t
bass	barn	pranc*e*	wa*s*	sco*a*t
brass	yarn	lanc*e*	wast	halt
class	bar	glanc*e*	*k*nob	salt
glass	far	tranc*e*	swab	malt
grass	scar	scarf	wad	fa*u*lt
arch	spar	last	dodg*e*	va*u*lt
march	star	swa⁵p	lodg*e*	fals*e*
parch	tar	dock	bodg*e*	bronz*e*
starch	*c*zar	mock	podg*e*	do⁶om
harsh	car	clock	foss*e*	room
charg*e*	char	*k*nock	bond	boom

loom	pool	noo*se*	shoot	roof
bloom	spool	choo*se*	book	loof
groom	droop	lo*se*	cook	soon
wom*b*	scoop	boo*se*	hook	hoop**
tom*b*	troop	ooze	look	coop
broom	loop	o*use*	took	poop
spoon	soup	coo	brook	full
boon	group	two	crook	bull
moon	hoop*	do	flook	pull
noon	boot	sho*e*	rook	wool
loon	coot	loo	shook	bush
swoon	hoot	woo	crou*p*	push
bo*urn*	toot	proof	wood	puss
poor	moot	woof	stood	e²*arl*
to*ur*	food	loo*se*	good	pe*arl*
moor	rood	goo*se*	hood	skirt***
boor	brood	moo*se*	co*uld*	ver*se*
cool	mood	spoon	wo*uld*	fier*ce*
fool	mo*ve*	roost	sho*uld*	pier*ce*
tool	pro*ve*	ro⁷ot	wolf	tier*ce*
stool	groo*ve*	foot	hoof	her*se*
ter*se*	quirk	so⁸n	spirt	sle*y*
ver*ge*	*h*erb	run	squirt	pre*y*
ser*ge*	verb	ton	kirk	gre*y*
dir*ge*	fir	won	work	we*igh*
vir*ge*	myrr*h*	done	bird	*eigh*
vert	fern	one****	word	ne*igh*
term	*e*arn	com*e*	first	re*ig*n
firm	ye*arn*	som*e*	worst	ve*in*
germ	le*arn*	bom*b*	worse	fe*ig*n
sperm	stern	clom*b*	on*ce**	foil
stirp	kern	rhom*b*	monk	boil
chirp	quern	dirt	tong*ue*	coil
jerk	se*arch*	shirt	birch	join
perk	perch	flirt	spon*ge*	coin
smerk	swer*ve*	wort	*h*e⁹ir	loin
yerk	wert	girt	trey	groin

*To cry out.   **Of a cask

***Under this figure, in the words skirt, &c. i has the sound of second e.

****Pronounced wun.   *Pronounced wunce.

boy	shout	blood	weight	cow
joy	spout	flood	streight	how
toy	scout	fir	tete	bow
coy	doubt	sir	feint	mow
cloy	browse	her	veil	sow
buoy	spouse	stir	**oi and oy**	vow
point	drowse	worm	oil	bout
joint	cloud	world	spoil	drought
voice	crowd	front	soil	our
brow	loud	wont	broil	sour
plow	proud	dove	toil	brown
bough	shroud	love	choice	crown
slough	bound	shove	moist	down
out	hound	glove	hoist	drown
stout	pound	twirl	joist	frown
oust	round	dunce	noise	clown
trout	sound	deign	quoit	gown
gout	ground	skein	coif	town
pout	wound	rein	quoif	house
clout	foul	eight	**ou and ow**	louse
rout		freight	now	mouse
douse	cowl	ounce	vouch	lounge
owl	growl	pounce	slouch	
fowl	howl	flounce	pouch	
scowl	bounce	couch	gouge	

MONOSYLLABLES IN TH.

The following have the first sound of th, viz. as in thick, thin.

thr¹ow	thowl	hath	breadth	bath
truth	threw	rath	filth	lath
youth	thrice	pith	frith	wrath
sheath	thrive	with*	plinth	thro⁵b
heath	throne	theft	spilth	throng
both	throe	thatch	tha³w	thong
oath	throve	thill	cloth	to⁶oth
forth	thi²ng	thrid	moth	through
fourth	think	thrill	broth	e²arth
highth	thin	thrush	sloth	dearth
three	thank	thwak	troth	birth
throat	thick	tilth	north	girth
theme	thrift	withe	loth	mirththi⁸rd
thigh	thumb	doth	thought	thirst
thief	thump	smith	thorn	worth
faith	length	thrust	froth	month
blowth	strength	thrum	thrall	thirl
growth	breath	thread	thwart	**ou**
quoth	death	stealth	warmth	south
ruth	health	thrash	swath	mouth
teeth	wealth	depth	pa⁴th	drouth
thane	threat	width	hearth	

*In this word, th has its first sound before a consonant, as in withstand; and its second sound before a vowel, as in without, with us. But in other compound words, th generally retains the sound of its primitive.

The following have the second sound of th, as in thou.

thi[1]ne	teeth*	blithe	then	the[9]y
thy	those	wreath	thus	there
bathe	tithe	writhe	them	their
lathe	these	scythe	thence	**ou**
swathe	though	seethe	than	thou
clothe	thee	breathe	bo[6]oth	mouth
loathe	hithe	thi[2]s	smooth	
meethe	lithe	that	soothe	

Examples of the formation of plurals, and other derivatives.

bay, bays	stain, stains	saint, saints
day, days	brain, brains	heap, heaps
lay, lays	chain, chains	tear, tears
pay, pays	pain, pains	hear, hears
pray, prays	paint, paints	spear, spears
sway, sways	claim, claims	creed, creeds
way, ways	strait, straits	trait, traits
mail, mails	plague, plagues	chief, chiefs
nail, nails	key, keys	leak, leaks
sail, sails	knave, knaves	speak, speaks
weep, weeps	green, greens	sheaf, sheaves
seam, seams	yield, yeilds	leaf, leaves

fly, flies	flight, flights	snow, snows
cry, cries	light, lights	hoe, hoes
dry, dries	sight, sights	foal, foals
stride, strides	life, lives	bowl, bowls
guide, guides	wife, wives	rogue, rogues
smile, smiles	knife, knives	post, posts
poll, polls	toe, toes	host, hosts
soul, souls	foe, foes	toast, toasts
coal, coals	bow, bows	coast, coasts
sky, skies	glow, glows	door, doors
buy, buys	flow, flows	floor, floors
sigh, sighs	blow, blows	oar, oars

*The noun teeth, has the first sound of th, and the verb to teeth its second sound. The same is observable of mouth and to mouth. This is the reason why these words are found under both heads.

The words mouth, moth, cloth, oath, path, swath, bath, lath, have the first sound of th in the singular number, and the second in the plural.

TABLE XIII.

Lessons of easy words, to teach children to read, and to know their duty.

LESSON I.

NO man may put off the law of God.
My joy is in His law all the day.
O may I not go in the way of sin!
Let me not go in the way of ill men.

II.

A bad man is a foe to the law;
It is his joy to do ill.
All men go out of the way.
Who can say he has no sin?

III.

The way of man is ill.
My son do as you are bid:
But if you are bid, do no ill.
See not my sin, and let me not go to the pit.

IV.

Rest in the Lord, and mind His word.
My son, hold fast the law that is good.
You must not tell a lie, nor do hurt.
We must let no man hurt us.

V.

Do as well as you can, and do no harm.
Mark the man that doth well, and do so too.
Help such as want help, and be kind.
Let your sins past put you in mind to mend.

VI.

I will not walk with bad men, that I may not be cast off with them.
I will love the law and keep it.
I will walk with the just and do good.

VII.

This life is not long; but the life to come has no end.
We must pray for them that hate us.
We must love them that love not us.
We must do as we like to be done to.

VIII.

A bad life will make a bad end.
He must live well that will die well.
He doth live ill that doth not mend.
In time to come we must do no ill.

IX.

No man can say that he has done no ill.
For all men have gone out of the way.
There is none that doth good, no not one.
If I have done harm, I must do it no more.

X.

Sin will lead us to pain and woe.
Love that which is good and shun vice.
Hate no man, but love both friends and foes.
A bad man can take no rest, day nor night.

XI.

He who came to save us, will wash us from all sin; I will be glad in His name.

A good boy will do all that is just; he will flee from vice; he will do good, and walk in the way of life.

Love not the world, nor the things that are in the world; for they are sin.

I will not fear what flesh can do to me; for my trust is in Him who made the world:

He is nigh to them that pray to Him, and praise His name.

XII.

Be a good child; mind your book; love your school, and strive to learn.

Tell no tales; call no ill names; you must not lie, nor swear, nor cheat, nor steal.

Play not with bad boys; use no ill words at play; spend your time well; live in peace, and shun all strife. This is the way to make good men love you, and save your soul from pain and woe.

XII.

A good child will not lie, swear, nor steal.

He will be good at home, and ask to read his book; when he gets up he will wash his hands and face clean; he will comb his hair, and make haste to school; he will not play by the way, as bad boys do.

XIV.

When good boys and girls are at school, they will mind their books, and try to learn to spell and read well, and not play in the time of school.

When they are at church, they will sit, kneel, or stand still; and when they are at home, will read some good book, that God may bless them.

XV.

As for those boys and girls that mind not their books, and love not the church and school, but play with such as tell tales, tell lies, curse, swear and steal, they will come to some bad end, and must be whipped till they mend their ways.

TABLE XIV.

Words of two syllables accented on the first.

a¹ cr*e*	fe male	*o*at me*a*l	trai tor
a pron	fro *w*ard	past ry	trea ty
bare foot	grate ful	pi *o*us	we*a* ry
be*a*st ly	gr*ie*v ous	pe*o* pl*e*	woe ful
brew er	*g*no mon	plu mag*e*	*w*ri ter
b*eau* ty	hain *o*us	pa rent	wain scot
brok *e*n	hind most	pro log*ue*	*y*e*o* man
bo*a*t swa*i*n	hoar y	quo ta	a²b sence
bo*w* sprit	hu mor	r*h*u barb	ab bey
brave ry	jew el	ri fl*e*	am pl*e*
ca bl*e*	jui cy	rog*u* ish	as*th* ma
che*a*p *e*n	*k*nave ry	re g*i*on	an kl*e*
dai ly	*k*night hood	se*a* *s*on	bal anc*e*
dai *s*y	li ver	spri*gh*t ly	bel fry
de*a* con	la bor	sti fl*e*	bash ful
di*a* mond	le g*i*on	stee pl*e*	bish op
do tag*e*	may or	bol ster	blem ish
eve ning	me ter	co*u*l ter	blus ter
fa vor	mi ter	slave ry	brim ston*e*
fla vor	me*a* *s*les	sho*u*l der	brick kiln
fe*a* ture	ni ter	tai lor	blud ge*o*n

bel lows	deunk ard	jour nal	quick en
bis cuit	dust y	judge ment	ram ble
brit tle	ec logue	knuck le	rap id
buck ram	en gine	knap sack	rat tle
bus tle	en sign	lan guage	reb el
cam el	en trails	lan guor	rel ish
cap rice	er ror	land lord	rig or
cap tain	fash ion	lev el	ris en
cen sure	fam ish	lim it	riv er
chap el	fas set	lus ter	riv et
chas ten	fat ten	lunch eon	ruf fle
cher ish	fes ter	mad am	res in
chim ney	fer riage	mal ice	sam ple
car ry	fid dle	man gle	sal mon
car riage	flag on	mas tiff	satch el
cis tern	frec kle	mel on	scab bard
cit y	frus trate	mer it	scis sors
clam or	fur lough	min gle	seven night
clean ly	fran chise	mis tress	scep ter
cred it	ges ture	mis chief	spec ter
crev ice	gant let	musk et	scrib ble
crick et	glis ten	mus lin	scuf fle
crust y	grand eur	mus ter	sin ew
crys tal	grav el	mar riage	sim ple
cup board	grum ble	nev er	sin gle
cus tom	guin ea	nim ble	skep tic
crib bage	gud geon	pad lock	smug gle
cul ture	hand ful	pamph let	span gle
cous in	hab it	pen ance	spig ot
cut lass	has soc	pes ter	spit tle
dam age	hav oc	pis mire	spin dle
dam ask	heif er	plan et	sup ple
dam sel	heav y	pleas ant	subt le
dam son	hin drance	peas ant	stur geon
dan gle	hus band	pin chere	sur geon
dac tyl	hum ble	prat tle	tal ent
debt or	husk y	pun ish	tal on
dim ple	im age	puz zle	tan gle
dis tance	in stance	pic ture	tat tle
doub le	in ward	pur chase	tav ern
driv en	isth mus	prac tice	tempt er
dud geon	jeal ous	phthis ic	ten ant
dun geon	jin gle	punch eon	till age

tip pl*e*	mor tal	cock swain	boo by
tres pass	mor*t* gag*e*	con duit	wo⁷ol len
tr*ou*b le	na*ugh* ty	cop y	bush el
twink ling	saw yer	con trite	bo *s*om
trans port	tor ment	cof fin	bush y
trun che*o*n	wa ter	doc trine	worst ed
ven om	sa*u* cy	flor id	cush i*o*n
ven tur*e*	sa*u* cer	fon dl*e*	bul let
vint ag*e*	a⁴n s*w*er	for*e* he*a*d	bul lock
vis it	barb er	frol ic	bul ly
vis ag*e*	brac*e* let	fal chi*o*n	bul wark
vi*c*t *ua*ls	cart er	grog ram	butch er
veng*e* ance	cham ber	go*s* lin	coop er
ven*i s*on	craft y	hog*s* he*a*d	cuck oo
vin*e* yard	char c*oa*l	hom ag*e*	ve²r min
wel com*e*	flask et	*h*on est	ver dict
wed lock	gar land	*h*on or	ver ju*i*ce
wick ed	g*h*ast ly	*k*nowl edge	vir tu*e*
*w*ran gl*e*	gar ment	hal lo*w*	kern el
*w*rap per	har lot	lodg er	co⁸n jur*e*
*w*res tl*e*	har vest	mod est	cov er
*w*rist band	ja*u*n dic*e*	mod ern	cir c*ui*t
we*a*p on	mark et	mon str*ou*s	fir kin
wid ge*o*n	mas ter	nov el	com pass
ze*a*l ot	mar quis	nov ice	com fort
zeal *o*us	par c*e*l	prof fer	bor *ou*gh
zeph yr	par d*o*n	prog ress	dirt y
sla³*ugh* ter	par lor	prom is*e*	gov ern
bor der	part ner	pros pect	hon *ey*
cor ner	pas tur*e*	pros per	sov*e* re*ig*n
da*ugh* ter	*psal*m ist	quad rant	stir rup
a*u* tum*n*	scar let	quad rate	skir mish
fa*u*lt y	slan der	squad ron	shov *e*l
for tress	a⁵l so	stop pag*e*	squir rel
for tune	al way	spon dee	vir gin
ga*u* dy	bon fire	wan der	wor ship
geor gic	cob ler	wan ton	won der
gorg*e o*us	clos et	war rant	ne⁹*igh* bor
la*u* rel	col l*e*ag*u*e	squan der	**ou**
lord ship	com et	yon der	coun cil
ha*ugh* ty	com rad*e*	gloo⁶m y	coun ter
morn ing	con qu*e*r	wo man	coun ty

dou*gh* ty	show er	pow er
drow sy	flow er	**oy**
moun t*a*in	bow er	voy age

TABLE XV.

LESSON I.

THE time will come when we must all be laid in the dust.

Keep thy tongue from ill, and thy lips from guile. Let thy words be plain and true to the thoughts of the heart.

He that strives to vex or hurt those that sit next him, is a bad boy, and will meet with foes – let him go where he will; but he that is kind, and loves to live in peace, will make friends of all that know him.

A clown will not make a bow, nor thank you when you give him what he wants; but he that is well bred, will do both.

He that speaks loud in school will not learn his own book well, nor let the rest learn theirs; but those that make no noise will soon be wise, and gain much love and good will.

II.

Shun the boy that tells lies, or speaks bad words; for he would soon bring thee to shame.

He that does no harm shall gain the love of the whole school; but he that strives to hurt the rest, shall gain their ill will.

He that lies in bed when he should go to school, is not wise; but he that shakes off sleep shall have praise.

He is a fool that does not choose the best boys when he goes to play; for bad boys will cheat, and lie, and swear, and strive to make him as bad as themselves.

Slight no man, for you know not how soon you may stand in need of his help.

III.

If you have done wrong, own your fault; for he that tells a lie to hide it, makes it worse.

He that tells the truth is a wise child; but he that tells lies, will not be heard when he speaks the truth.

When you are at school, make no noise, but keep your seat, and mind your book; for what you learn will do you good, when you grow to be a man.

Play no tricks on them that sit next you; for if you do, good boys will shun you as they would a dog that they knew would bite them.

He that hurts you at the same time that he calls you his friend, is worse than a snake in the grass.

Be kind to all men, and hurt not thyself.

A wise child loves to learn his book, but the fool would choose to play with toys.

IV.

Sloth keeps such a hold of some boys, that they lie in bed when they should go to school; but a boy that wants to be wise will drive sleep far from him.

Love him that loves his book, and speaks good words, and does no harm: For such a friend may do thee good all the days of thy life.

Be kind to all as far as you can; you know not how soon you may want their help; and he that has the good will of all that know him shall not want a friend in time of need.

If you want to be good, wise and strong, read with care such books as have been made by wise and good men; think of what you read in your spare hours; be brisk at play, but do not swear; and waste not too much of your time in bed.

TABLE XVI.

Words of two syllables, accented on the second.

ac qui¹re	de pose	re straint	sub orn
a base	de scribe	re *s*ume	trans form
a bu*s*e	de sign	re tain	e cla⁴t
a *dieu*	de *s*ire	re *s*ign	ad vanc*e*
af fair	de vise	sup pose	a far
af fri*gh*t	dis claim	tran scribe	a larm
a gainst	dis c*our*se	trans po*s*e	*g*uit ar
a mu*s*e	dis may	un clo*s*e	in graft
ap pro*a*ch	dis own	un ti*e*	re mark
ar rai*g*n	dis play	un tru*e*	sur pass
a rise	dis po*s*e	up ri*gh*t	ca tarr*h*
as si*g*n	en close	ad jou²rn	re gard
a stra*y*	en cro*a*ch	a by*s*s	ap pro⁶ve
a vail	en de*a*r	at tack	a m*ou*r
a wake	en tre*a*t	at tempt	bab oon
a way	ex ci*s*e	a veng*e*	bas soon
al ly	ex po*s*e	ad ept	be hoove
aw ry	in cre*a*se	be head	buf foon
be l*i*eve	in di*c*t	be twixt	ca no*e*
be l*i*ef	im pair	bur les*que*	car t*ou*ch
benign	in fu*s*e	con tem*n*	dis prov*e*
be s*i*ege	in scribe	con tempt	a do
be lo*w*	ma li*g*n	co quet	a loof
be sto*w*	ob tain	e n*o*ugh	e me²rg*e*
bo he*a*	o pa*que*	fi ness*e*	im mers*e*
con si*g*n	ob lige	ga zette	af firm
com plain	per tain	gro tes*que*	de *s*ert
cam pai*g*n	pre vail	har ang*ue*	de *s*erve
com po*s*e	pre scribe	im men*s*e	a bo⁸ve
con di*g*n	pro po*s*e	qua drill*e*	a mong
con cise	pur su*i*t	so journ	be com*e*
con ce*i*t	pro ro*gue*	be ca³*us*e	be lov*e*
con fu*s*e	re ce*i*ve	a dorn	con ve⁹*y*
con strain	re ce*i*pt	a broad	sur ve*y*
de ce*i*ve	re c*our*se	de fraud	in ve*igh*
de ce*i*t	re pair	de bau*ch*	**oi**
de cre*a*se	re po*s*e	per form	ap point
de li*gh*t	re prieve	re ward	a noint

a void	re joic*e*	com pound	pro pound
em broil	sub join	con found	sur mount
en joy	dis joint	de vour	al low
de story	**ou**	ac count	a bound
de coy	a mount	pro nounc*e*	an nounc*e*
pur loin	a bout	re nounc*e*	ca rous*e*

TABLE XVII.

Examples of words derived from their roots or primitives.

EXAMPLE I.

Prim.	Deriv.	Prim.	Deriv.	Prim.	Deriv.
rain	rain-y	grass	grass-y	froth	froth-y
rust	rust-y	glass	glass-y	hair	hair-y
leaf	leaf-y	ice	i-cy	size	si-zy
stick	stick-y	frost	frost-y	chill	chill-y
pith	pith-y	snow	snow-y	chalk	chalk-y
length	length-y	fog	fog-gy	down	down-y
slight	slight-y	wood	wood-y	gloss	gloss-y
storm	storm-y	room	room-y	worth	wor-thy

EXAMPLE II.

Plural nouns of two syllables, formed from the singular of one syllable.

lace	la-ces	brush	brush-es	house	hous-es
face	fa-ces	price	pri-ces	church	church-es
pace	pa-ces	slice	sli-ces	box	box-es
trace	tra-ces	spice	spi-ces	tierce	tier-ces
cage	ca-ges	grace	gra-ces	verse	vers-es
page	pa-ges	press	press-es	lodge	lodg-es
nose	no-ses	dress	dress-es	watch	watch-es
rose	ro-ses	maze	ma-zes	noise	nois-es
curse	curs-es	fish	fish-es	voice	voic-es
purse	purs-es	horse	hors-es	charge	charg-es
surge	surg-es	corpse	corps-es	sense	sens-es
loss	loss-es	cause	caus-es	fringe	frin-ges
arch	arch-es	farce	far-ces	ridge	ridg-es
cheese	chees-es	course	cours-es	dance	dan-ces

EXAMPLE III.

Words formed by adding ing to verbs, and called Participles.

call	call-ing	al-lay	al-lay-ing
air	air-ing	com-plain	com-plain-ing
faint	faint-ing	al-low	al-low-ing
feel	feel-ing	fin-ish	fin-ish-ing
see	see-ing	lav-ish	lav-ish-ing
beat	beat-ing	glim-mer	glim-mer-ing

Words in which e final is omitted in the derivative.

change	chang-ing	ex-change	ex-chang-ing
glance	glanc-ing	dis-pose	dis-pos-ing
prance	pranc-ing	gen-er-ate	gen-e-rat-ing
grace	grac-ing	con-verse	con-vers-ing
give	giv-ing	con-vince	con-vinc-ing
hedge	hedg-ing	op-e-rate	op-e-ra-ting
style	styl-ing	dis-solve	dis-solv-ing
solve	solv-ing	im-i-tate	im-i-tat-ing
tri-fle	tri-fling	re-ceive	re-ceiv-ing
ri-fle	ri-fling	per-ceive	per-ceiv-ing
shuf-fle	shuf-fling	prac-tice	prac-tic-ing

EXAMPLE IV.

The manner of expressing degrees of comparison in qualities, by adding er and est, or r and st; called Positive, Comparative, and Superlative.

Pos.	Comp.	Super.	Pos.	Comp.	Super.
great	great-er	great-est	wise	wis-er	wis-est
kind	kind-er	kind-est	ripe	rip-er	rip-est
bold	bold-er	bold-est	rare	rar-er	rar-est
rich	rich-er	rich-est	grave	grav-er	grav-est
near	near-er	near-est	chaste	chast-er	chast-est
cold	cold-er	cold-est	brave	brav-er	brav-est
warm	warm-er	warm-est	vile	vil-er	vil-est

EXAMPLE V.

Words ending in ish, expressing a degree of quality less than the positive.

red-dish	red	red-der	red-dest
brown-ish	brown	brown-er	brown-est
whi-tish	white	whi-ter	whit-est
green-ish	green	green-er	green-est
black-ish	black	black-er	black-est
blu-ish	blue	blu-er	blu-est
yel-low-ish	yel-low	yel-low-er	yel-low-est

EXAMPLE VI.

Formation of verbs in the three persons.

Present Time

Singular		Plural
I love, thou lovest you love	he loveth he loves she loves it loves	We love ye or you love they love
I grant, thou grantest, you grant	he granteth he grants she grants it grants	We grant ye or you grant

Past Time

I loved, thou lovedst you loved	he loved she loved it loved	We loved you or you loved they loved

TABLE XVIII.

Familiar Lessons.

A Dog growls and barks; a cat mews and purrs; a cock crows; a hen clucks and cackles; a bird chirps and sings; an ox lows; a bull bellows; a lion roars; a horse neighs; an ass brays; a whale spouts. Birds fly in the air by the help of wings; snakes crawl on the earth without feet; fishes swim in water, by means of fins; beasts have feet, with hoofs or claws, to walk or run on land.

All animals are fitted for certain modes of living. The birds which feed on flesh, have strong claws, to catch and hold small animals, and a hooked bill to tear the flesh in pieces; such is the vulture and the hawk. Fowls which feed on insects and grain, have mostly a short strait bill, like the robin. Those which live on fish, have long legs for wading, or long bills for seizing and holding their prey, like the heron and fish hawk. Fowls which delight chiefly to fly in the air, and light and build nests on the trees, have their toes divided, by which they cling to the branches and twigs; those which live in and about water have webbed feet, that is, their toes united by a film or skin, so that their feet serve as oars or paddles for swimming.

See the dog, the cat, the wolf, the lion, the panther and catamount; what sharp claws and pointed teeth they have, to seize little animals, and tear them in pieces! But see the gentle cow and ox, and timid sheep – these useful animals are made for man – they have no claws, nor sharp teeth; they have only blunt teeth in the under jaw, fitted to crop the grass of the field; they feed in quiet, and come at the call of man. Oxen submit to the yoke, and plow the field, or draw the cart; the cow returns home at evening, to fill the farmer's pails with milk, the wholesome food of men; and the sheep yields her yearly fleece, to furnish us with warm garments.

Henry, tell me the number of days in a year. Three hundred and sixty-five. How many weeks in a year? Fifty-two. How many days in a week? Seven. What are they called? Sunday, Monday, Tuesday, Wednesday, Thursday, Friday, Saturday: Sunday is the Sabbath, or day of rest, and called the Lord's day, being devoted to religious duties. How many hours are there in a day? Twenty-four. How many minutes in an hour? Sixty, and sixty seconds in a minute. Time is measured by clocks and watches, dials and glasses. The light of the sun makes the day, and the shade of the earth makes the night. The earth is round, and rolls round from west to east once in twenty-four hours. The day time is for labor, and the night for sleep and repose. Children should go to bed early.

Charles, how is the year divided? Into months and seasons. How many are the months? Twelve calendar months, and nearly thirteen lunar months. What are the names of the calendar months? January, February, March, April, May, June, July, August, September, October, November, December. January begins the year, and the first day of that month is called New Year's day. Then people express to each other their good wishes, and little boys and girls expect gifts of little books, toys and plums. What is the lunar month? It is the time from one change of the moon to another, which is about twenty-nine days, and a half.

John, what are the seasons? Spring, summer, autumn or fall, and winter. The spring is so called from the springing or first shooting of the plants; when they put forth leaves and blossoms, all nature is decked with bloom, and perfumed with fragrant odors. The spring months are March, April and May. The summer months are June, July and August, when the sun pours his heating rays on the earth, the trees are clothed with leaves and fruit, and the ground is covered with herbage. The autumnal months are September, October and November; which are also called fall, from the fall of the leaves. Now the fruits are gathered, the verdure of the plants decays; the leaves of the forest turn red or yellow, and fall from the trees, and nature is stripped of her verdant robes. Then comes dreary winter. In December, January and February, frost binds the earth in chains, and spreads an icy bridge over rivers and lakes: the snow, with her white mantle, enwraps the earth; no birds fill the air with the music of their notes; the beasts stand shivering in the stall: and men crowd around the fire-side, or wrapped in wool and fur, prepare to meet the chilling blast.

ADVICE

Prefer solid sense to vain wit; study to be useful rather than diverting; commend and respect nothing so much as true piety and virtue. Let no jest intrude to violate good manners; never utter what may offend the chastest ear.

TABLE XIX.

Words of three syllables, the full accent on the first, and the half accent on the third.

Note. In half accented terminations, ate, ude, ure, ize, ute, ise, ule, uge, ide, the vowel has its first sound generally, though not dwelt upon so long, or pronounced with so much force as in the full accented syllables.

But in the terminations ice, ive, ile, the vowel has generally its second sound, and the final e is superfluous, or only softens c; as notice, relative, juvenile, – pronounced notis, relativ, juvenil. In the former case, the final e is in Roman; and in the latter case, in Italic.

di¹ a phra*g*m	al ti tude	el o quenc*e*
du pli cat*e*	ab dic ate	el e vate
di a lo*gue*	ac cu rate	em pha sis
aid de camp	ad e quate	em u l*o*us
e go ti*s*m	ac tu ate	en ter prize
fa vor it*e*	ag o nize	en vi *o*us
for ci bl*e*	al ge bra	ep i cure
fre quen cy	am or *o*us	es ti mate
fu gi tiv*e*	an ec dote	ex cel lenc*e*
fe*a* *s*i bl*e*	an ti quate	fas ci nate
glo ri *o*us	ap ti tude	fab u l*o*us
he ro i*s*m	an o dyne	feb ri fuge
ju bi lee	ap er ture	fluc tu ate
ju ve nil*e*	as y lum	fur be lo*w*
live li hood	bev e rage	gen er *o*us
lu bri cate	blun der buss	gen tl*e* man
lu cra tiv*e*	cat a log	gen u in*e*
lu dic r*o*us	cal cu late	grad u ate
ni*gh*t in gale	can di date	gran a ry
nu mer *o*us	can dl*e* stick	hem i sphere
o di *o*us	car a way	hes i tate
pre vi *o*us	cel e brate	hand ker chie*f*
pa gan ism	crit i ci*s*m	hur ri cane
pl*eu* ri sy	cim e tar	hyp o crit*e*
*rh*eu ma ti*s*m	c*o*urt e sy	im ag*e* ry
ru min ate	cul ti vate	im pi *o*us
scru pu l*o*us	dec a lo*gue*	in fa m*o*us
se ri *o*us	dec o rate	in sti gate
spu ri *o*us	ded i cate	in sti tute
su i cide	def i nit*e*	in ti mate
su*i*t a bl*e*	del e gate	je*a*l *o*us y
va ri *o*us	dem on strate	je*o*p ar dy
u ni form	der o gate	jes sa min*e*
u *s*u ry	des o late	las si tude
a²d jec tiv*e*	des po ti*s*m	lat i tude
ag gra vate	des pe rate	lib er tin*e*
an a pest	des ti tute	lit i gate
an im ate	dem a go*gue*	mack er el
ap pe tite	ep *au* lett*e*	mag ni tude
	ep i lo*gue*	man u script

mas sa cre	rev er end	for tu nate
med i cine	rhap so dy	lau da ble
med i tate	rhet o ric	plau si ble
mis chiev ous	rid i cule	por phy ry
met a phor	sac ri fice	a[4]rch i tect
musk mel on	sac ri lege	ar gu ment
nour ish ment	sal i vate	ar ma ment
ped a gogue	sas sa fras	ar ti fice
pal li ate	sat i rize	bay o net
pal pa ble	scav en ger	bar ba rism
pal pi tate	sens i ble	bar ba rous
par a ble	sep a rate	car di nal
par a dise	ser a phim	car pen ter
par a digm	stadt hold er	chan cel lor
par a phrase	stim u late	chan ce ry
par a site	stip u late	guar di an
par ent age	stren u ous	ghast li ness
par ox ysm	sub ju gate	lar ce ny
par ri cide	sub se quent	mar gin al
pen te cost	sub sti tute	mas quer ade
per quis ite	syn a gogue	par ti san
phys i cal	sim i le	phar ma cy
plen i tude	skep ti cism	par lia ment
pres by ter	syn co pe	rasp ber ry
pres i dent	sur ro gate	a[5]l der man
pris on er	syc o phant	al ma nac
priv i lege	syl lo gism	bot a ny
quer u lous	tan ta lize	col lo quy
par a sol	tan ta mount	com pli ment
rail le ry	tel e scope	com plai sance
ran cor ous	ten a ble	con sti tute
rap tur ous	tim o rous	con tem plate
rav en ous	treach er ous	com pen sate
rec ti tude	trip li cate	con fis cate
rel a tive	tur pi tude	cor o ner
ren o vate	vas sal age	crock e ry
re qui site	vin di cate	hor i zon
ren dez vous	bil let doux	lon gi tude
rep ro bate	fra[3]ud u lent	nom i nate
res i dence	cor di al	ob li gate
res i due	cor po ral	ob lo quy
ret i nue	for feit ure	ob sta cle
rev er ence	for ti tude	ob sti nate

ob vi *o*us

om i n*o*us

op e rate

op po *s*ite

or i fice

prob a bl*e*

pop u l*o*us

po*s* i tiv*e*

pot en tate

prof li gate

proph e cy

quar an tine

pros e cute

por rin ger

pros per *o*us

pros ti tute

sol e ci*s*m

sol i tude

soph is try

vol a tile

roq *ue* l*au*r

tom a hawk

pe²r se cute

per son age

prin ci pl*e*

serv i tude

ter mi nate

firm a ment

mir a cl*e*

ci⁸r cu lar

cir cum stanc*e*

cir cum spect

com pa ny

com*e* li ness

gov ern or

gov ern ess

oi

poig nan cy

roy al ty

ou

coun sel lor

coun ter f*ei*t

coun te nanc*e*

boun ti ful

TABLE XX.

LESSON I.

MY son, hear the counsel of thy father, and forsake not the law of thy mother.

If sinners entice thee to sin, consent thou not.

Walk not in the way with them; refrain thy feet from their path, for their feet run to evil, and make haste to shed blood.

II.

Be not wise in thine own eyes; but be humble.

Let truth only proceed from thy mouth. Despise not the poor, because his is poor; but honor him who is honest and just. Envy not the rich but be content with thy fortune. Follow peace with all men, and let wisdom direct thy steps.

III.

Happy is the man that findeth wisdom. She is of more value than rubies. Length of days is in her right hand, and in her left hand, riches and honor. Her ways are pleasant, and all her paths are peace. Exalt her and she shall promote thee. She shall bring thee to honor, when thou dost embrace her.

IV.

The ways of virtue are pleasant, and lead to life; but they who hate wisdom, love death. Therefore pursue the paths of virtue and peace, that safety and glory will by thy reward. All my delight is upon the saints that are in the earth, and upon such as excel in virtue.

TABLE XXI.

Words of three syllables, accented on the second.

a chie¹v ment	ad ven ture	ex ces sive
ac quaint ance	af fran chise	ex pen sive
ap prais er	ag grand ize	ex pres sive
ar rear age	dis fran chise	ex ten sive
blas phe mer	ap pren tice	ex cheq uer
con ta gion	au tum nal	es cutch eon
con ta gious	bis sex tile	ho san na
cor ro sive	com pul sive	il lus trate
cour age ous	cur mud geon	i am bus
de ceit ful	con jec ture	in cen tive
de ci sive	con vul sive	in cul cate
dif fu sive	de ben ture	in den ture
in qui ry	de fect ive	in jus tice
e gre gious	dis cour age	in vec tive
en light en	dis par age	lieu ten ant
o bei sance	dis sem ble	mo men tous
out rage ous	ef ful gent	of fen sive
pro ce dure	en tan gle	op pres sive
po ta to	ex cul pate	mis pris ion
so no rous	gym nas tic	pneu mat ics
mus ke toe	ef fect ive	pre sump tive
a bri²dge ment	em bez zle	pro duc tive
ac knowl edge	en deav or	pro gres sive

re pul siv*e*   im pos tur*e*   a po^{5}s tl*e*

re ten tiv*e*   per for manc*e*   re mon strat*e*

re venge ful   re cord er   sub al tern

r*h*eu mat ic   mis for tun*e*   ac co^{6}*u* ter

stu pen d*o*us   ad va^{4}n tag*e*   ma n*e*u ver

sub mis siv*e*   a part ment   al te^{2}r nate

ab o^{5}r tiv*e*   de part ment   de ter mine

in dors*e* ment   di*s* as ter   re h*ea*r sal

im por tanc*e*   em bar go   sub ver siv*e*

The following are accented on the first and third syllables.

ap per ta^{1}in   con n*oi*s s*e*ur   em bra *s*ure

ad ver ti*s*e   dis ap p*ea*r   ac qui e^{2}s*ce*

as cer tain   en ter tain   co a les*ce*

con tra vene   gaz et teer   mal*e* con tent

can non ade   deb o nair   coun ter ma^{4}nd

TABLE XXII.

Words not exceeding three syllables, divided.

LESSON I.

The wick-ed flee when no man pur-su-eth; but the right-e-ous are as bold as a li-on.

Vir-tue ex-alt-eth a na-tion; but sin is a re-proach to a-ny peo-ple.

The law of the wise is a foun-tain of life to de-part from the snares of death.

Wealth got-ten by de-ceit, is soon wast-ed; but he that gath-er-eth by la-bor, shall in-crease in rich-es.

II.

I-dle-ness will bring thee to pov-er-ty; but by in-dus-try and pru-dence thou shalt be filled with bread.

Wealth mak-eth ma-ny friends; but the poor are for-got-ten by their neigh-bors.

A pru-dent man fore-seeth the e-vil, and hid-eth him-self; but the thought-less pass on and are pun-ished.

III.

Train up a child in the way he should go, and when he is old he will not de-part from it.

Where there is no wood the fire go-eth out, and where there is no tat-ler the strife ceas-eth.

A word fit-ly spok-en is like ap-ples of gold in pic-tures of sil-ver.

He that cov-er-eth his sins shall not pros-per, but he that con-fess-eth and for-sak-eth them shall find mer-cy.

IV.

The rod and re-proof give wis-dom; but a child left to him-self bring-eth his par-ents to shame.

Cor-rect thy son, and he will give thee rest; yea he will give thee de-light to thy soul.

A man's pride shall bring him low; but hon-or shall up-hold the hum-ble in spir-it.

The eye that mock-eth at his fath-er, and scorn-eth to obey his moth-er, the ra-vens of the val-ley shall pick it out, and the young ea-gles shall eat it.

V.

By the bless-ing of the up-right, the cit-y is ex-alt-ed, but it is o-ver-thrown by the mouth of the wick-ed.

Where no coun-sel is, the peo-ple fall; but in the midst of coun-sel-lors there is safe-ty.

The wis-dom of the pru-dent is to un-der-stand his way, but the fol-ly of fools is de-ceit.

A wise man fear-eth and de-part-eth from e-vil; but the fool rag-eth and is con-fi-dent.

Be not hast-y in thy spir-it to be an-gry; for an-ger rest-eth in the bo-som of fools.

TABLE XXIII.

Words of four syllables, accented on the first.

a²d mi ra bl*e*	mar ri*age* a bl*e*	vul ner a bl*e*
ac cu rate ly	mis er a bl*e*	a¹ mi a bl*e*
am i ca bl*e*	nav i ga bl*e*	ju di ca ture
ap pli ca bl*e*	pal li a tiv*e*	va ri a bl*e*
ar ro gant ly	pit i a bl*e*	ho⁵s pit a bl*e*
cred it a bl*e*	pref er a bl*e*	for mid a bl*e*
crim in al ly	ref er a bl*e*	a⁴n swer a bl*e*
des pi ca bl*e*	rev o ca bl*e*	co⁵m mon al ty
el i gi bl*e*	sump tu *o*us ly	nom in a tiv*e*
es ti ma bl*e*	spec u la tiv*e*	op er a tiv*e*
ex pli ca tiv*e*	suf fer a bl*e*	prof it a bl*e*
fig u ra tiv*e*	tem per a ture	tol er a bl*e*
lam ent a bl*e*	val u a bl*e*	cop u la tiv*e*
lit er a ture	ven er a bl*e*	

The following have the half accent on the third syllable.

a²g ri cul tur*e*	tab er na cl*e*	a⁴rch i tect ur*e*
an ti qua ry	tran sit o ry	ar bi tra ry
ap o plex y	a³*u* dit o ry	par si mo ny

TABLE XXIV.

Words of four syllables; the full accent on the second, and half accent on the fourth.

Note. The terminations ty, ry, and ly, have very little accent.

60 *An Easy Standard of Pronunciation.*

ad vi[1] sa ble	am big u ous	pa rish on er
ac cu mu late	am phib i ous	re cep ta cle
ap pro pri ate	a nal y sis	ri dic u lous
an ni hi late	ar tic u late	si mil i tude
a me na ble	as sas si nate	sus cep ti ble
ab bre vi ate	be at i tude	tem pest u ous
al le vi ate	ca lum ni ate	tu mult u ous
cen so ri ous	ca pit u late	vi cis si tude
com mo di ous	cer tif i cate	vo cif er ous
com mu ni cate	ca tas tro phe	vo lup tu ous
con cu pis cence	co ag u late	u nan i mous
com pa ra ble	com bus ti ble	de ba[3]uch e ry
de plo ra ble	com mem o rate	con form i ty
dis pu ta ble	com mis er ate	de form i ty
er ro ne ous	com par a tive	e nor mi ty
har mo ni ous	com pat i ble	sub or di nate
im me di ate	com pend i ous	a bo[5]m i nate
im pe ri ous	con grat u late	ac com mo date
im pla ca ble	con spic u ous	a non y mous
in tu i tive	con tem pla tive	a poc a lypse
la bo ri ous	con tempt i ble	a poc ry pha
me lo di ous	con tig u ous	a pos tro phe
mys te ri ous	de fin i tive	cor rob o rate
no to ri ous	de lib er ate	de nom i nate
ob se qui ous	de riv a tive	de mon stra ble
op pro bri ous	di min u tive	de pop u late
pe nu ri ous	e phem er is	dis con so late
pre ca ri ous	e piph a ny	pre pos ter ous
sa lu bri ous	fa cil it ate	pre rog a tive
spon ta ne ous	fa nat i cism	re spons i ble
ter ra que ous	il lus tri ous	ad mi[2]s si ble
vi ca ri ous	im pet u ous	con vers a ble
vic to ri ous	in dus tri ous	re vers i ble
vo lu min ous	in gen u ous	su per flu ous
ux o ri ous	in quis i tive	su per la tive
as pa[2]r a gus	in vid i ous	pre serv a tive
ac cel er ate	in vin ci ble	ac co[8]m pa ny
ad mis si ble	in vis i ble	dis cov er y
ad ven tur ous	per fid i ous	**oi**
a dul ter ate	per spic u ous	em broid er y
ac cept a ble	pre dic a ment	
ag gran dize ment	per plex i ty	
dis fran chise ment	pro mis cu ous	

TABLE XXV.

THERE are five states of human life, infancy, childhood, youth, manhood, and old age. The infant is helpless; he is nourished with milk. When he has teeth, he begins to eat bread, meat, and fruit, and is very fond of cakes and plums. The little boy chooses some plaything that will make a noise, a hammer, a stick, or a whip. The little girl loves her doll and learns to dress it. She chooses a closet for her baby-house, where she sets her doll in a little chair, by the side of a table, furnished with tea-cups as big as a thimble.

As soon as boys are large enough, they run away from home, grow fond of play, climb trees to rob birds' nests, tear their clothes, and when they come home, their parents often chastise them. O how the rod makes their legs smart. These are naughty boys, who love play better than their books, cruel boys, who rob the birds of their eggs – poor little birds which do no harm, which fill the air with the sweet melody of their notes, and do much good by devouring the worms, and other insects, which destroy the fruits and herbage.

Charles, how many barley corns make an inch? Three. How many feet in a yard? Three. How many yards in a rod, perch, or pole? Five and a half. How many rods in a mile? Three hundred and twenty. How many rods in a furlong? Forty. How many furlongs in a mile? Eight. How many miles in a league? Three. How many lines in an inch? Twelve. What is a cubit? The length of the arm from the elbow to the end of the longest finger, which is about eighteen inches. A fathom is the distance of the ends of a man's fingers, when the arms are extended, which is about six feet.

Henry, tell me the gills in a pint. Four. Two pints make a quart, four quarts make a gallon. Barrels are of various sizes; some contain no more than twenty-seven gallons, some thirty, or thirty-two, others thirty-six. A hogshead contains sixty-three gallons; but we usually call puncheons by the name of hogsheads, and these hold about one hundred and ten gallons. A pipe contains two hogsheads, or four barrels, or about one hundred and twenty gallons.

TABLE XXVI.

Words of five syllables; the full accent on the second.

co te²m po ra ry	de fam a to ry
de clam a to ry	dis pens a to ry

e lec tu a ry

e pis to la ry

ex clam a to ry

ex plan a to ry

ex tem po ra ry

he red i ta ry

in cen di a ry

in flam ma to ry

pre lim i na ry

com mu¹ ni ca bl*e*

com mu ni ca tiv*e*

in vi o la bl*e*

per spi ra to ry

de ge²n er a cy

con fed er a cy

con sid er a bl*e*

pre par a to ry

pro hib i to ry

re *s*id u a ry

tu mult u a ry

vo cab u la ry

vo lup tu a ry

con so⁵l a to ry

de po*s* i to ry

de rog a to ry

in vol un ta ry

re po*s* i to ry

ob *s*e²rv a to ry

de lib er a tiv*e*

ef fem in a cy

in suf fer a bl*e*

in dis so lu bl*e*

in vul ner a bl*e*

in vet er a cy

in ter min a bl*e*

in tem per ate ly

TABLE XXVII

WILLIAM, tell me how many mills make a cent? Ten. How many cents a dime? Ten. Tell me the other coins of the United States. Ten dimes make a dollar, ten dollars an eagle, which is a gold coin, and the largest which is coined in the United States. Dimes and dollars are silver coins. Cents are copper coins. These are new species of coin. What is the ancient manner of reckoning money? By pounds, shillings, pence and farthings. Four farthings make a penny, twelve pence a shilling, and twenty shillings a pound.

William loves fruit. See him picking strawberries – bring him a basket – let him put the berries in a basket, and carry them to his mama and sisters. Little boys should be kind and generous – they should always carry some fruit home for their friends. Observe the cherry trees – see, how they begin to redden – in a few days, the cherries will be ripe, the honey-hearts, the black-hearts, and ox-hearts, how sweet they are. You must not eat too many, and make yourself sick. Fill your basket with cherries and give them to your little friends.

Now see the pears. The harvest pear, how yellow. It is ripe, let me pick and eat it. The sugar pear, how plump and soft it is; and what a beautiful red covers one side of it. See the catherine pear, and the vergaloo, how rich, juicy, and delicious. But the peach – how it exceeds all fruit in its delicious flavor; what can equal its fragrance, and how it melts upon the tongue. The nutmeg, the rare-ripe with its blushing cheek, the white cling-stone with its crimson tints, and the lemon cling-stone with its golden hue, and all the varieties of the free stones. Such are the rich bounties of nature, bestowed on man to please his taste, preserve his health, and draw his grateful heart towards the Author of his happiness.

REMARKS

A wise man will consider, not so much the present pleasure and advantage of a measure, as its future consequences.
Sudden and violent passions are seldom durable.

TABLE XXVIII.

Words of five syllables accented on the first and third.

am bi gu[1] i ty
con ti gu i ty
con tra ri e ty
dic ta to ri al
ep i cu re an
im por tu ni ty
no to ri e ty
op por tu ni ty
per pe tu i ty
per spi cu i ty
pres by te ri an
pri mo ge ni al
su per flu i ty
tes ti mo ni al
ac a de[2]m i cal
af fa bil i ty
al pha bet i cal
an a lyt i cal
ar gu ment a tive
mon o syl la ble
plau si bil i ty
pol y syl la ble
pop u lar i ty

pos si bil i ty
pri mo gen i ture
prin ci pal i ty
prob a bil i ty
prod i gal i ty
punc tu al i ty
pu sil lan i mous
reg u lar i ty
rep re hen si ble
rep re sen ta tive
sat is fac to ry
sen si bil i ty
sen su al i ty
sim i lar i ty
sin gu lar i ty
tes ta ment a ry
cir cum am bi ent
com pre hen si ble
con san guin i ty
con tra dict o ry
cred i bil i ty
di a met ri cal
el e men ta ry

ep i dem i cal

e van gel i cal

fal li bil i ty

gen e al o gy

hos pi tal i ty

il le git i mate

im per cep ti bl*e*

in tel lec tu al

in tro duc to ry

in tre pid i ty

ir re *s*ist i bl*e*

mag na nim i ty

met a phy*s* i cal

an a to⁵m i cal

an i mos i ty

a pos tol i cal

ar is toc ra cy

a tro nom i cal

cat e gor i cal

cu ri os i ty

di a bol i cal

et y mol o gy

gen e ros i ty

e qui pon der ant

in dis solv a bl*e*

in ter rog a tiv*e*

met a phor i cal

pe ri od i cal

phi lo soph i cal

phy*s* i og no my

phy*s* i ol o gy

trig o nom e try

u ni form i ty

u ni ve²rs i ty

em blem at i cal

ge o graph i cal

TABLE XXIX.

LESSON I.

BE not anxious for your life, what ye shall eat, or what ye shall drink; nor for your body, what ye shall put on; for your heavenly Father knoweth that ye have need of these things.

Behold the fowls of the air: For they sow not, neither do they reap, nor gather into barns; yet your heavenly Father feedeth them.

Consider the lilies of the field, how they grow; they toil not, neither do they spin; and yet Solomon in all his glory, was not arrayed like one of these.

II.

Therefore be not anxious for the good things of this life, but seek first the kingdom of heaven and its righteousness, and all these things shall be added to you.

Ask and it shall be given unto you; seek and ye shall find; knock, and it shall be opened.

Love your enemies; bless them that curse you; do good unto them that hate you; and pray for them that scornfully use you and persecute you.

III.

When thou prayest, be not as the hypocrites, who love to pray standing in the synagogues, and in the streets, that they may be seen of men: But when thou prayest, enter into thy closet, and when thou hast shut thy door, pray to thy Father who is in secret, and thy Father who seeth in secret shall reward thee openly.

IV.

Lay not up for yourselves treasures on earth, where moth and rust doth corrupt, and where thieves break through and steal; but lay up for yourselves treasures in heaven, where neither moth nor rust doth corrupt, and where thieves do not break through and steal: For where your treasure is, there will your heart be also.

Our Savior's Golden Rule.

ALL things which you would have men do to you, do ye the same to them; for this is the law and the prophets.

TABLE XXX.

In the following words tion, tian, tial and tier, are pronounced chun, chal, chur.

co^1*ur* tier	fus tian	com bus tion
b^{2}as tion	mix tion	di ges tion
chris tian	ce le^{2}s tial	ad mix tion

And in all words where t is preceded by s or x.

In all other words tion is pronounced shun; as are also cion, cyon, sion. Thus, motion, coercion, halcyon, mansionare pronounced moshun, coershun, halshun, manshun. Cial is pronounced shal.

Words of two syllables accented on the first.

mo^1 tion	fac tion	pen sion
na tion	fic tion	sanc tion
lo tion	frac tion	sec tion
por tion	fric tion	ses sion
po tion	func tion	ten sion
ra tion	man sion	unc tion
sta tion	men tion	a^3*uc* tion
a^{2}c tion	mis sion	o^{5}p tion
dic tion	pas sion	ve^{2}r sion

Words of three syllables accented on the second.

ces sa^1 tion	at ten tion	ex pres sion
com mo tion	col lec tion	in flic tion
de vo tion	com mis sion	ob jec tion
plan ta tion	com pres sion	pro fes sion
pol lu tion	con fes sion	pro tec tion
pro por tion	con sum*p* tion	pre em*p* tion
re la tion	con ven tion	re dem*p* tion
sal va tion	con vic tion	re flec tion
fi du cial	cor rec tion	sub jec tion
ad mi^{2}s sion	de cep tion	suc ces sion
af fec tion	de scrip tion	sus pen sion
af flic tion	di rec tion	as per sion
as cen sion	dis tinc tion	as ser tion
as sum*p* tion	ex cep tion	a ver sion

con ver sion dis per sion sub ver sion
de ser tion re ver sion sub stan tial

Words of four syllables; the full accent on the third, and the half accent on the first.

ac cept a^1 tion nav i ga tion
ac cu *s*a tion ob ser va tion
ad mi ra tion per se cu tion
ad o ra tion pre*s* er va tion
ag gra va tion proc la ma tion
ap pro ba tion pub li ca tion
av o ca tion ref or ma tion
cal cu la tion re*s* o lu tion
con dem na tion rev e la tion
con gre ga tion sep a ra tion
con sti tu tion sup pli ca tion
con tem pla tion trib u la tion
cul ti va tion vi o la tion
dec la ra tion vi*s* i ta tion
des o la tion ap pre^2 hen sion
ed u ca tion com pre hen sion
el o cu tion con de *sc*en sion
em u la tion con tra dic tion
ex pec ta tion ju ris dic tion
hab i ta tion res ur rec tion
in cli na tion sat is fac tion
in sti tu tion a^3*u*g men ta tion
med i ta tion a^{5}l ter a tion
mod e ra tion

Words of five syllables, accented on the first and fourth.

am pli fi ca^1 tion ci^{8}r cum lo cu tion
qual i fi ca tion cir cum val la tion
ed i fi ca tion co^{5}m mem mo ra tion
as so ci a tion con fed e ra tion
mul ti pli ca tion con grat u la tion
con tin u a tion con so ci a tion
rat i fi ca tion or gan i za tion
sanc ti fi ca tion co^1 op e ra tion
sig ni fi ca tion glo ri fi ca tion

pro nun ci a tion	re nun ci a tion
pro pi ti a tion	re tal i a tion
re gen e ra tion	ar gu men ta tion

Note. As-sas-si-na-tion, de-nom-i-na-tion, de-ter-mi-na-tion, il-lu-mi-na-tion, have the second and fourth syllables accented, and tran-sub-stan-ti-a-tion, has an accent on the first, third and fifth syllables. Con-sub-stan-ti-a-tion, follows the same rule.

TABLE XXXI.

Familiar Lessons.

HENRY is a good boy. Come here, Henry, let me hear you read. Can you spell easy words? Hold up your head; speak loud and plain. Keep your book clean; do not tear it.

John, keep your seat, and sit still. You must not say a word, nor laugh nor play. Look on your book, learn your letters, study your lesson.

Charles, can you count? Try. One, two, three, four, five, six, seven, eight, nine, ten. Well said; now spell bird. B-i-r-d. How the birds sing and hop from branch to branch among the trees. They make nests too, and lay eggs; then sit on their eggs, and hatch young birds. Dear little birds, how they sing and play. You must not rob their nests, nor kill their young: it is cruel.

Moses, see the cat, how quiet she lies by the fire. Puss catches mice. Did you ever see puss watching for mice? How still and sly! She creeps along, fixing her eyes steady on the place where the mouse lies. As soon as she gets near enough, she darts forward, and seizes the little victim by the neck. Now the little mouse will do no more mischief.

See the little helpless kittens. How warm and quiet they lie in their bed, while puss is gone. Take them in your hands, don't hurt them; they are harmless, and do no hurt. They will not bite nor scratch. Lay them down softly, and let them go to sleep.

George, the sun has risen, and it is time for you to rise. See the sun, how it shines: it dispels the darkness of night, and makes all nature gay and cheerful. Get up, Charles; wash your hands, comb your hair, and get ready for breakfast. What are we to have for breakfast? Bread and milk. This is the best food for little boys. Sometimes we have coffee or tea, and toast. Sometimes we have cakes.

James, hold your spoon in your right hand; and if you use a knife and fork, hold the knife in your right hand. Do not eat fast: hungry boys are apt to eat fast, like the pigs.

Never waste your bread; bread is gained by the sweat of the brow. Your father plants or sows corn; corn grows in the field; when it is ripe, it is cut, and put in the barn; then it is thrashed out of the ears, and sent to a mill: the mill grinds it, and the bolter separates the bran from the flour. Flour is wet with water or milk; and with a little yeast or leaven, it is raised, and made light; this is called dough: dough is baked in an oven, or pan, and makes bread.

THE SISTERS.

Emily, look at the flowers in the garden. What a charming sight. How the tulips adorn the borders of the alleys, dressing them with gaiety. Soon the sweet pinks will deck the beds; and the fragrant roses perfume the air. Take care of the sweet-williams, the jonquils, and the artemisia. See the honey-suckle, how it winds about the column, and climbs along the margin of the windows. Now it is in bloom, how fragrant the air around it; how sweet the perfume, after a gentle shower, or amidst the soft dews of the evening. Such are the charms of youth, when robed in innocence; such is the bloom of life, when decked with modesty, and a sweet temper. Come, my child, let me hear your song.

The Rose.

The rose had been wash'd, lately wash'd in a show'r,
that Julia to Emma convey'd;
A plentiful moisture encumber'd the flow'r,
And weigh'd down its beautiful head.

The cup was all filled, and the leaves were all wet,
And seem'd at a fanciful view,
To weep with regret, for the buds it had left,
On the flourishing bush where it grew.

I hastily seiz'd it, unfit as it was
For a nosegay, so dripping and drown'd;
And shaking it rudely, – too rudely, alas,
I snapt it – it fell to the ground.

"And such," I exclaimed, "is the pitiless part
Some act by the delicate mind;
Regardless of wringing and breaking a heart

Already to sorrow resign'd.

"This beautiful rose, had I shaken it less,
Might have bloom'd with the owner a while;
And the tear that is wip'd, with a little address,
May be follow'd perhaps with a smile."

Julia, rise in the morning betimes, dress the borders of the flower beds, pull up the noxious weeds, water the thirsty roots. See how the plants wither for want of rain. The flowers fade, the leaves shrivel and droop. Bring a little water to refresh them. Now the plants look green and fresh; the weeds which shaded or robbed their roots of moisture, are removed, and the plants will thrive. Does the heart want culture? Weed out the noxious passions from the heart, as you would hurtful plants from among the flowers. Cherish the virtues – love, kindness, meekness, modesty, goodness. Let them thrive, and produce their natural fruit, pure happiness, and joys serene through life.

Look to the gentle lambs, how innocent and playful; how agreeable to the sight; how pleasant the task to feed them; how grateful they are for your care. Julia, let me hear your song.

The Lamb.

A young feeble Lamb, as Emily pass'd,
In pity she turned to behold;
How it shiver'd and shrunk from the merciless blast,
Then fell all benumb'd with the cold.

She rais'd it, and touch'd with the innocent's fate,
Its soft form to her bosom she prest;
But the tender relief was afforded too late,
It bleated, and died on her breast.

The moralist then, as the corse she resign'd
And weeping, spring flow'rs o'er it laid,
Thus mus'd, "So it fares with the delicate mind,
To the tempest of fortune betray'd.

"Too tender, like thee, the rude shock to sustain,

And deni'd the relief which would save,
She's lost, and when pity and kindness are vain,
Thus we dress the poor sufferer's grave."

Harriet, bring your book, let me hear you read. What book have you? Let me see: a little volume of poems. How many can you repeat? Let me hear my dear Harriet speak one.

The Bird's Nest

Yes, little nest, I'll hold you fast,
And little birds, one, two, three, four;
I've watch'd you long, you're mine at last;
Poor little things, you'll 'scape no more.

Chirp, cry, and flutter, as you will,
Ah! simple rebels, 'tis in vain;
Your little wings are unfledg'd still,
How can you freedom then obtain?

What note of sorrow strikes my ear?
Is it their mother thus distrest?
Ah yes and see, their father dear
Flies round and round, to seek their nest.

And is it I who cause their moan?
I, who so oft in summer's heat,
Beneath yon oak have laid me down
To listen to their songs so sweet?

If from my tender mother's side,
Some wicked wretch should make me fly,
Full well I know, 'twould her betide,
To break her heart, to sink, to die.

And shall I then so cruel prove,
Your little ones to force away!
No, no; together live and love;

See here they are, – take them, I pray.

Teach them in yonder wood to fly,
And let them your sweet warbling hear,
Till their own wings can soar as high,
And their own notes may sound as clear.

Go, gentle birds; go free as air;
While oft again in summer's heat,
To yonder oak I will repair,
And listen to your songs so sweet.

Mary, what a charming little sonnet your sister Harriet has repeated. Come, my sweet girl, you must let me hear what you can say. But stop, let me see your work. Your little fingers are very handy with a needle. Very pretty indeed; very pretty work. What small stitches. You shall hem and mark all your papa's handkerchiefs, and very soon you shall work a muslin frock for yourself. Now, my girl, let me hear you repeat some verses.

On a Goldfinch starved in his Cage.

Time was when I was free as air,
The thistle's downy seed my fare,
My drink the morning dew;
I perch'd at will on every spray,
My form genteel, my plumage gay,
My strains for ever new.

But gaudy plumage, sprightly strain,
And form genteel, were all in vain,
And of a transient date;
For caught and cag'd, and starv'd to death,
In dying sighs, my little breath
Soon pass'd the wiry grate.

Thanks, little Miss, for all my woes,
And thanks for this effectual close,
And cure of ev'ry ill;
More cruelty could none express,
And I, if you had shown me less,

Had been your pris'ner still.

Precepts concerning the social relations.

ART thou a young man, seeking for a partner for life? Obey the ordinance of God, and become a useful member of society. But be not in haste to marry, and let thy choice be directed by wisdom.

Is a woman devoted to dress and amusement? Is she delighted with her own praise, or an admirer of her own beauty? Is she given to much talking and loud laughter? If her feet abide not at home, and her eyes rove with boldness on the faces of men – turn thy feet from her, and suffer not thy heart to be ensnared by thy fancy.

But when thou findest sensibility of heart joined with softness of manners; an accomplished mind and religion, united with sweetness of temper, modest deportment, and a love of domestic life – Such is the woman who will divide the sorrows, and double the joys of thy life. Take her to thyself; she is worthy to be thy nearest friend, thy companion, the wife of thy bosom.

Art thou a young woman, wishing to know thy future destiny? Be cautious in listening to the addresses of men. Art thou pleased with smiles and flattering words? Remember that man often smiles and flatters most, when he would betray thee.

Listen to no soft persuasion, till a long acquaintance and a steady, respectful conduct have given thee proof of the pure attachment and honorable views of thy lover. Is thy suitor addicted to low vices? is he profane? is he a gambler? a tipler? a spendthrift? a haunter of taverns? has he lived in idleness and pleasure? has he acquired a contempt for thy sex in vile company? And above all, is he a scoffer at religion? – Banish such a man from thy presence; his heart is false, and his hand would lead thee to wretchedness and ruin.

Art thou a husband? Treat thy wife with tenderness and respect; reprove her faults with gentleness; be faithful to her in love; give up thy heart to her in confidence, and alleviate her cares.

Art thou a wife? Respect thy husband; oppose him not unreasonably, but yield thy will to his, and thou shalt be blest with peace and concord; study to make him respectable, as well for thine own sake, as for his; hide his faults; be constant in thy love; and devote thy time to the care and education of the dear pledges of thy love.

Art thou a parent? Teach thy children obedience; teach them temperance, justice, diligence in useful occupations; teach them science; teach them the social virtues, and fortify thy precepts by thine own example; above all teach them religion. Science and virtue will make them respectable in this life – religion and piety alone can secure to them happiness in the life to come.

Art thou a brother or a sister? Honor thy character by living in the bonds of affection with thy brethren. Be kind; be condescending. Is thy brother in adversity, assist him; if thy sister is in distress, administer to her necessities and alleviate her cares.

Art thou a son or a daughter? Be grateful to thy father, for he gave thee life; and to thy mother, for she sustained thee. Piety in a child is sweeter than the incense of Persia, yea more delicious than odors, wafted, by western gales, from a field of Arabian spices. Hear the words of thy father for they are spoken for thy good; give ear to the admonitions of thy mother, for they proceed from her tenderest love. Honor their gray hairs, and support them in the evening of life; and thine own children, in reverence of thy example, shall repay thy piety with filial love and duty.

FABLE I.

Of the Boy that stole Apples.

AN old man found a rude boy upon one of his trees stealing Apples, and desired him to come down; but the young Sauce-box told him plainly he would not. "Won't you?" said the old Man. "Then I will fetch you down." So he pulled up some tufts of Grass, and threw at him; but this only made the Youngster laugh, to think the old Man should pretend to beat him down from the tree with grass only.

"Well, well," said the old Man, "if neither words nor grass, will do, I must try what virtue there is in Stones," so the old man pelted him heartily with stones; which soon made the young Chap hasten down from the tree and beg the old Man's pardon.

MORAL.

If good words and gentle means will not reclaim the wicked, they must be dealt with in a more severe manner.

TABLE XXXII.

In all words ending in ow unaccented, w is silent, and o has its first sound. Many of these words are corrupted in vulgar pronunciation; follow is called foller, &c. for which reason the words of this class are collected in the following table.

ba²r row	cal low	whit low
bel low	mal lows	wid ow
bil low	mar row	wil low
bur row	mead ow	win dow
el bow	mel low	win now
fel low	min now	yel low
fal low	nar row	bo⁵r row
far row	hol low	fol low
fur row	shad ow	mor row
gal lows	shal low	sor row
bel lows	spar row	wal low
har row	tal low	swal low

TABLE XXXIII.

In the following words, si sounds like zh. Thus, confusion is pronounced confu-zhun; bra-sier, bra-zhur; o-zier, o-zhur; vi-sion, vizh-un; plea-sure, plea-zhur.

Note. In this and the following table, the figures show the accented syllables, without any other direction.

bra¹ sier	de lu sion	oc ca sion
cro sier	dif fu sion	ob tru sion
gla zier	ef fu sion	vi² sion
o zier	ex clu sion	mea sure
ra sure	ex plo sion	plea sure
ho sier	e va sion	trea sure
sei zure	a bra sion	lei sure
fu sion	cor ro sion	a zure
am bro sial	de tru sion	ab sci² sion
ad he sion	dis plo sion	col li sion
al lu sion	in clo sure	con ci sion
co he sion	e ro sion	di vi sion
col lu sion	il lu sion	de ci sion
con clu sion	in tru sion	de ri sion
con fu sion	in fu sion	e li sion
con tu sion	pro fu sion	e ly sian

| pre ci *s*ion | in ci *s*ion | re ci *s*ion |
| pro vi *s*ion | al li *s*ion | ci⁸r cum ci²s ion |

The compounds and derivatives follow the same rule.

FABLE II.

The country Maid and her Milk pail.

WHEN men suffer their imagination to amuse them, with the prospect of distant and uncertain improvements of their condition, they frequently sustain real losses, by their inattention to those affairs in which they are immediately concerned.

A country Maid was walking very deliberately with a pail of milk upon her head, when she fell into the following train of reflections: The money for which I shall sell this milk, will enable me to increase my stock of eggs to three hundred. These eggs, allowing for what may prove addle, and what may be destroyed by vermin, will produce at least two hundred and fifty chickens. The chickens will be fit to carry to market about Christmas, when poultry always bears a good price; so that by May day I cannot fail of having money enough to purchase a new gown. Green – let me consider – yes, green becomes my complexion best, and green it shall be. In this dress I will go to the fair, where all the young fellows will strive to have me for a partner; but I shall perhaps refuse every one of them, and with an air of disdain toss from them. Transported with this triumphant thought, she could not forbear acting with her head what thus passed in her imagination, when down came the pail of milk, and with it all her imaginary happiness.

TABLE XXXIV.

Words in which cie, sie, and tie are pronounced she; tia and cia, sha; cious and tious, shus. Thus ancient, partial, captious, are pronounced, anshent, parshal, capshus. This rule will be sufficient to direct the learner to a right pronunciation, without distinguishing the silent letters.

Gre¹ cian	quo tient	spe cies*
gra cious	spa cious	so cial
pa tient	spe cious	sa tiate

*Pronounced speshiz. The compounds and derivatives follow the same rule.

An Easy Standard of Pronunciation. 77

a^{2}n cient   fal la cious   po ten tial

cap tious   fe ro cious   pro vin cial

fac tious   in gra tiate   pru den tial

fic tious   lo qua cious   sen ten tious

nup tial   ne go ciate   sub stan tiate

tran sient   pro ca cious   com me^{2}r cial

lus cious   ra pa cious   con tu ma^1 cious*

ca^{3}u tious   sa ga cious   ef fi ca cious

pa^{4}r tial   se qua cious   os ten ta tious

co^{5}n scienc*e*   te na cious   per spi ca cious

con scious   vex a tious   per ti na cious

ap pre^1 ciate   vi va cious   cir cum sta^{2}n tial

as so ciate   vo ra cious   con sci en tious

a*u* da cious   an nu^{2}n ciate   con se quen tial

ca pa cious   con ten tious   con fi den tial

con so ciate   cre den tials   pen i ten tial

dis so ciate   e nun ciate   pes ti len tial

e ma ciate   es sen tial   prov i den tial

ex cru ciate   in fec tious   rev e ren tial

ex pa tiate   li cen tiate   re*s* i den tia ry

fa ce tious   om nis cienc*e*   e qui noc tial

FABLE III.

The Fox and the Swallow.

ARISTOTLE informs us, that the following fable was spoken by Aesop to the Samians, on a debate upon changing their ministers, who were accused of plundering the commonwealth.

A Fox swimming across a river, happened to be entangled in some weeds that grew near the bank, from which he was unable to extricate himself. As he lay thus exposed to whole swarms of flies, which were galling him and sucking his blood, a swallow, observing his distress, kindly offered to drive them away. "By no means," said the Fox, "for if these should be chased away, which are already sufficiently gorged, another more hungry swarm would succeed, and I should be robbed of every remaining drop of blood in my veins."

*The words of four syllables have the half accent on the first.

TABLE XXXV.

In the following words the vowels are short, and the accented syllable must be pronounced as though it ended with the consonant sh. Thus, pre-cious, spe-cial, effi-cient, logi-cian, mili-tia, addi-tion, are pronounced presh-us, spesh-ul, effish-ent, logish-an, milish-a, addish-on. These words will serve as examples for the following table.

pre^2 cious	of fi ciate	er u di tion
spe cial	of fi cial	ex hi bi tion
vi cious	of fi cious	ex po si tion
vi tiate	pa tri cian	im po si tion
ad di^2 tion	par ti tion	op po si tion
am bi tion	per di tion	prej u di cial
a*u*s pi cious	per ni cious	pol i ti cian
ca pri cious	pe ti tion	prop o si tion
co mi tial	pro fi cient	prep o si tion
con di tion	phy *s*i cian	pro hi bi tion
cog ni tion	po *s*i tion	r*h*et o ri cian
con tri tion	pro pi tious	su per fi cial
de fi cient	se di tion	su per sti tion
de li cious	se di tious	sup po si tion
dis cre tion	sol sti tial	sur rep ti tious
dis cu tient	suf fi cient	av a ri cious
e di tion	sus pi cious	ben e fi c*i*al
ef fi cient	tran si tion	co a li tion
es pe cial	vo li tion	com pe ti tion
fla gi tious	ab o li^2 tion*	com po si tion
fru i *t*ion	ac qui *s*i tion	def i ni tion
ju di cial	ad mo ni tion	dem o li tion
lo gi cian	ad ven ti tious	dep o si tion
ma gi cian	am mu ni tion	dis po si tion
ma li cious	ap pa ri tion	prac ti^2 tion er
mi li tia	ar ti fi cial	a rith me ti^2 cian
mu *s*i cian	ad *sc*i ti tious	ac a de mi cian
nu tri tion	ap po *s*i tion	sup pos i ti tious
no vi ciate	eb ul li tion	math e ma ti cian

The compounds and derivatives follow the same rule.

*The words of four syllables have a half accent on the first, except practitioner. Arithmetician and supposititious have the half accent on the second, academician and mathematician on the first.

In the following words, the consonant q terminates a syllable: but perhaps the ease of the learner may render a different division more eligible.

e² qui ty	li que fy	in i qui ty
e qui ta ble	li qui date	in i qui tous
li quid	la quey	ob li qui ty
li quor	an ti qui ty	

SELECT SENTENCES

Never speak of a man's virtues to his face, nor of his faults behind his back; thus you will equally avoid flattery which is disgusting, and slander which is criminal.

If you are poor; labor will procure you food and clothing – if you are rich, it will strengthen the body, invigorate the mind, and keep you from vice. Every man therefore should be busy in some employment.

FABLE IV.

The Cat and the Rat.

A CERTAIN Cat had made such unmerciful havoc among the vermin of her neighborhood, that not a single Rat or Mouse dared venture to appear abroad. Puss was soon convinced, that if affairs remained in their present situation, she must be totally unsupplied with provision. After mature deliberation therefore, she resolved to have recourse to stratagem. For this purpose, she suspended herself from a hook with her head downwards, pretending to be dead. The Rats and Mice, as they peeped from their holes observing her in this dangling attitude, concluded she was hanging for some misdemeanor; and with great joy immediately sallied forth in quest of their prey. Puss, as soon as a sufficient number were collected together, quitting her hold, dropped into the midst of them and very few had the fortune to make good their retreat. This artifice having succeeded so well, she was encouraged to try the event of a second. Accordingly she whitened her coat all over, by rolling herself in a heap of flour, and in this disguise lay concealed in the bottom of a meal tub. This stratagem was executed in general with the same effect as the former. But an old experienced Rat, altogether as cunning as his adversary, was not so easily ensnared. "I don't much like," said he, "that white heap yonder; something whispers me there is mischief concealed under it. 'Tis true it may be meal; but it may likewise be something that I should not relish quite so well. There can be no harm at least in keeping at a proper distance; for caution, I am sure, is the parent of safety."

TABLE XXXVI.

In the following table, i before a vowel sounds like y at the beginning of words, as in junior, filial, dominion, which are pronounced junyur, filyal, dominyon.

fo¹l io	mill ion	in gen i*o*us
jun ior	min ion	bat ta²l ion
sol dier*	pill ion	ci vil ian
sav ior	pin ion	com pan ion
se*ig*n ior	trill ion	con nex ion
un ion	trunn ion	de flux ion
al ien	val iant	do min ion
gen ial	cull ion	fa mil iar
gen ius	runn ion	o pin ion
a²nx ious**	scull ion	pa vil ion
*b*dell ium	bull ion	post ill ion
bil ious	co⁵ll ier	punc till io
bill iards	pon iard	ras cal ion
bill ions	o⁸n ion	re bell ion
brill iant	be ha¹v i*o*ur	se ra*g*l io
ba*g*n io	com mun ion	ver mil ion
fil ial	par hel ion	a*u*x il ia ry
flex ion	pe cul ear	mi²n ia ture
flux ion	con ven ient	pe cu¹n ia ry

*Pronounced sol-ger.   **Pronounced ank-shus.

FABLE V.

The Fox and the Bramble.

A FOX, closely pursued by a pack of Dogs, took shelter under the covert of a Bramble. He rejoiced in this asylum; and for a while, was very happy; but soon found that if he attempted to stir, he was wounded by thorns and prickles on every side. However, making a virtue of necessity, he forbore to complain; and comforted himself with reflecting that no bliss is perfect; that good and evil are mixed, and flow from the same fountain. "These Briars, indeed," said he, "will tear my skin a little, yet they keep off the dogs. For the sake of the good then let me bear the evil with patience; each bitter has its sweet; and these Brambles, though they wound my flesh, preserve my life from danger."

TABLE XXXVII.

The first sound of th, as in think.

e^1 ther	the a ter	en thu *s*i a*s*m
ja cinth	hy a cinth	an ti^{2}p a thy
the sis	ca^{2}th o lic	pa renth e sis
zen ith	ep i thet	a rith me tic
thu^{2}n der	lab y rinth	an tith e sis
meth od	leth ar gy	mis an thro py
an them	pleth o ry	phi lan thro py
diph thong	sym pa thy	can thar i des
eth ics	am a ranth	the o^{5}c ra cy
pan ther	am e thyst	the ol o gy
sab bath	ap a thy	the od o lite
thim bl*e*	can the rus	ther mom e ter
this tl*e*	math e sis	au thor i ty
thur*s* day	syn the sis	ca thol i con
triph thong	pan the on	my thol o gy
en thra^{3}ll	e the^1 re al	or thog ra phy
ath wart	can tha ris	hy poth e sis
be troth	ca the dral	li thog ra phy
thi^{8}r ty	u re thra	li thot o my
thor o*ugh*	au the^{2}n tic	a poth e ca ry
thir te^{1}en	pa thet ic	ap o the^1 o sis
ou	syn thet ic	pol y the i*s*m
thou *s*and	a canth us	bib li o the^1 cal
a^1 the i*s*m	ath let ic	ich thy o^{5}l o gy
the o ry	me theg lin	or ni thol o gy
the o rem	ca tha^{4}r tic	

Second sound of th, as in thou.

e^1*i* ther	gath er	wheth er	thith er
ne*i* ther	hith er	neth er	whith er
he*a* then	le*a*th er	weth er	fa^4 ther
cloth ier	fur ther	prith ee	far thing
ra^{2}th er	breth ren	bur then	far ther
fath om	we*a*th er	*s*outh ern	po^{5}th er
fe*a*th er	with er	teth er	broth el

bro^{8}th er	smoth er	be que*a*th	lo^{5}g a rithm*s*
wor thy	oth er	an o^{8}th er	ne^{2}v er the le^{2}ss
moth er	be ne^{1}*a*th	to ge^{2}th er	

The derivatives follow the same rule.

FABLE VI.

The Bear and the Two Friends.

TWO Friends, setting out together upon a journey, which led through a dangerous forest, mutually promised to assist each other, if they should happen to be assaulted. They had not proceeded far, before they perceived a Bear making towards them with great rage.

There were no hopes in flight; but one of them, being very active, sprang up into a tree; upon which the other, throwing himself flat on the ground, held his breath and pretended to be dead; remembering to have heard it asserted, that this creature will not prey upon a dead carcase. The bear came up, and after smelling to him some time, left him, and went on. When he was fairly out of sight and hearing, the hero from the tree called out, "Well, my friend, what said the bear? He seemed to whisper you very closely." "He did so," replied the other, "and gave me this good piece of advice, never to associate with a wretch, who in the hour of danger, will desert his friend."

TABLE XXXVIII.

Words in which ch have the sound of k.

Chri^{1}st	te trarch	pas chal
chyle	cha os	cho^{5}l ic
scheme	cho ral	chol er
ache	e poch	schol ar
cha^{2}*s*m	o cher	mon arch
chri*s*m	tro chee	schi^{2}r r*o*us
cho^{5}rd	a^{2}n chor	sto^{8}m ach
loch	christ *e*n	pa^{1} tri arch
scho^{6}ol	chem ist	eu cha rist
oi	ech o	a^{2}n ar chy
choir	chal ic*e*	chrys o lite
cho^{1} rus	sched ule	char ac ter

cat e chism

pen ta t*e*uch

sep ul cher

tech ni cal

al chem y

an cho ret

brach i al

lach ry mal

mach i nate

sac cha rin*e*

syn chro nism

mich *a*el mas

cho⁵r is ter

chron i cl*e*

or ches ter

och i my

chi me¹ ra

pa ro chi al

cha mel ion

tri ba²c chus

chro mat ic

me chan ic

ca chex y

cha lib e ate

a nach ro nism

syn ec do chy

pry r*h*ich i us

am phib ri chus

me²l an chol y

chro no⁵l o gy

chi rog ra phy

chor eog ra phy

chro nom e ter

the om a chy

an ti ba²c chus

ca²t e che²t ic al

bac chan a¹l ian

cat e chu men

ich thy o⁵l ogy

FABLE VII.

The Two Dogs.

HASTY and inconsiderate connections are generally attended with great disadvantages; and much of every man's good or ill fortune, depends upon the choice he makes of his friends.

A good-natured Spaniel overtook a surly Mastiff, as he was traveling upon the high road. Tray, although an entire stranger to Tiger, very civilly accosted him; and if it would be no interruption, he said, he should be glad to bear him company on his way. Tiger, who happened not to be altogether in so growling a mood as usual, accepted the proposal; and they very amicably pursued their journey together. In the midst of their conversations, they arrived at the next village, where Tiger began to display his malignant disposition, by an unprovoked attack upon every dog he met. The villagers immediately sallied forth with great indignation, to rescue their respective favorites; and falling upon our two friends, without distinction or mercy, poor Tray was most cruelly treated, for no other reason, but his being found in bad company.

TABLE XXXIX.

Words of French origin, in which ch sound like sh, and i, accented, like e long.

cha[1]ise	in trig*ue*	bomb a *s*in
cha[2]m ois*	ma rine	man da rin
chan cr*e*	der nier	brig a di*er*
cham a[1]de	po lic*e*	bom bard i*er*
cham paign	ma chin*e* ry	buc can i*er*
fra ch*e*ur	che[2]v er il	can non i*er*
chi cane	chev is ance	cap a pi*e*
piq*u*[10]e	chiv al ry	car bin i*er*
shire	deb a*u* che[1]e	cav a li*er*
ma chi[10]ne	chev a li[10]er	cor de li*er*
cash i*er*	chan de lier	gren a di*er*
an tiq*ue*	cap u chin	fi nan ci*er*
fa tig*ue*	mag a zine	

SELECT SENTENCES

We may as well expect that God will make us rich without industry, as that He will make us good and happy, without our own endeavors.

Zeno, hearing a young man very loquacious, told him, that men have two ears and but one tongue; therefore they should hear much and speak little.

A man who, in company, engrosses the whole conversation, always gives offense; for the company consider him as assuming a degree of superiority, and treating them all as his pupils.

The basis of all excellence in writing and conversation, is truth – truth is intellectual gold, which is as durable as it is splendid and valuable.

Faction seldom leaves a man honest, however it may find him.

*Pronounced shammy.

FABLE VIII.

The Partial Judge.

A FARMER came to a neighboring Lawyer, expressing great concern for an accident which he said had just happened. "One of your Oxen," continued he, "has been gored by an unlucky Bull of mine, and I should be glad to know how I am to make you reparation." "Thou art a very honest fellow," replied the Lawyer, "and wilt not think it unreasonable that I expect one of thy Oxen in return." "It is no more than justice," quoth the Farmer, "to be sure; but what did I say? – I mistake – It is your Bull that has killed one of my Oxen." "Indeed!" says the Lawyer, "that alters the case: I must inquire into the affair; and if" – "and if!" said the Farmer, "the business I find would have been concluded without an if, had you been as ready to do justice to others, as to exact it from them."

TABLE XL.

Words in which g is hard before e, i, and y.

ge^1*ar*	dag ger	leg ged	g*h*er kin
geese	crag gy	pig gin	a^3*u* ger
ge^{2}ld	bug gy	quag gy	bo^{5}g gy
get	crag ged	rag ged	fog gy
gift	dig ger	rig ger	clog gy
giv*e*	dreg gy	rig gish	cog ger
gig	drug get	rug ged	dog ged
gild	drug gist	scrag ged	dog ger
gill	flag gy	scrag gy	dog gish
gimp	gib ber	shag gy	jog ger
gi^{8}rd	gib bous	slug gish	nog gen
girt	gid dy	snag ged	pa^{4}r get
girl	gig gl*e*	sprig gy	tar get
ea ger	gig let	stag ger	gi^{8}r dle
me*a* ger	giz zard	swag ger	be gi^{2}n
gew gaw	gim blet	swag gy	wa^{2}g ge ry
ti ger	hag gish	trig ger	lo^{5}g ger he*ad*
to ged	jag gy	twig gin	or gi^{2}l l*ous*
bi^{2}g gin	jag ged	twig gy	to geth er
brag ger	*k*nag gy	wag gish	pe^{2}t ti fo^{5}g ger

The following are pronounced as though they were written with double g. Thus, finger is pronounced fing-ger.

fi²n ger	lin ger	young er	long est
an ger	lin go	young est	strong er
hun ger	lin guist	long er	mo⁸ng er

These with their compounds and derivatives, are most of the words in the language, in which g has its hard sound before e, i, and y. But to these must be added the derivatives of verbs ending in g. Thus from dig come diggeth, diggest, digged, digging, &c. in which g is hard before e and i.

TABLE XLI.

The Boy that went to the Wood to look for Birds' Nests, when he should have gone to School.

WHEN Jack got up, and put on his clothes, he thought if he could get to the wood he should be quite well; for he thought more of a bird's nest, than his book, that would make him wise and great. When he came there, he could find no nest, but one that was on the top of a tree, and with much ado he got up to it, and robbed it of the eggs. Then he tried to get down; but a branch of the tree found a hole in the skirt of his coat, and held him fast. At this time he would have been glad to be at school; for the bird in a rage at the loss of her eggs, flew at him, and was like to pick out his eyes. Now it was that the sight of a man at the foot of the tree, gave him more joy than all the nests in the world. This man was so kind as to chase away the bird, and help him down from the tree; and from that time forth he would not loiter from school; but grew a good boy and a wise young man; and had the praise and good will of all that knew him.

OBSERVATIONS

The cheerful man hears the lark in the morning; the pensive man hears the nightingale in the evening.

He who desires no virtue in a companion, has no virtue himself; and that state is hastening to ruin, in which no difference is made between good and bad men.

Some men read for the purpose of learning to write; others, for the purpose of learning to talk – the former study for the sake of science; the latter, for the sake of amusement.

TABLE XLII.

It is a rule in the language, that c and g are hard at the end of words, and they commonly are so at the end of syllables; but in the following table they are soft, like s and j at the end of the accented syllable. Thus, magic, acid, are pronounced majic, asid, and ought to be divided mag-ic, ac-id. It is a matter disputed by teachers which is the most eligible division – mag-ic, ac-id, or ma-gic, a-cid. However, as children acquire a habit of pronouncing c and g hard at the end of syllables, I choose not to break the practice, but have joined these consonants to the last syllable. The figures show that the vowels of the accented syllables are all short.

ma² gic	re gi cide	au da ci ty
tra gic	re gi men	ca pa ci ty
a gil*e*	re gi ment	fu ga ci ty
a cid	re gis ter	lo qua ci ty
di git	spe ci fy	men da ci ty
vi gil	spe ci men	men di ci ty
fa cil*e*	ma cer ate	di la cer ate
fra gil*e*	ma ci lent	du pli ci ty
fri gid	ma gis trate	fe li ci ty
ri gid	ne ces sa ry	mu ni ci pal
pla cid	tra ge dy	an ti ci pate
pi g*eo*n	vi ci nage	par ti ci pate
si gil	ve ge tate	sim pli ci ty
ta cit	ve ge tant	me di ci nal
a gi tate	lo⁵ gic	so li ci tude
ag ge rate*	pro cess	per ni ci ty
le gi bl*e*	co gi tate	tri pli ci ty
fla gel late	pro ge ny	ver ti ci ty
pre ce dent	il li² cit	e da ci ty
pre ci pic*e*	im pli cit	ex ag ger ate
re ci pe	e li cit	mor da ci ty
de ci mal	ex pli cit	nu ga ci ty
de ci mate	so li cit	o pa ci ty
la cer ate	im a gine	ra pa ci ty
pa ci fy	re li g*io*n	sa ga ci ty
pa ge*a*nt ry	li ti g*iou*s	se qua ci ty
pa gi nal	pro di g*iou*s	vi va ci ty

The compounds and derivatives follow the same rule.

*g soft.

te na ci ty	o le a gi n*ous*	fe ro ci ty
ve ra ci ty	au then ti ci ty	ve lo ci ty
a da gi o	e las ti ci ty	r*h*i no ce ros
bel li ger ent	e lec tri ci ty	an a lo⁵ gi cal
or i gi nal	du o de ci mo	as tro lo gi cal
ar mi ger *ous*	ab o ri gi nal	ge o lo gi cal
om ni gi n*ous*	ec cen tri ci ty	ped a go gi cal
ver ti gi n*ous*	mu cil a gin *ous*	phi lo lo gi cal
re fri ger ate	mul ti pli ci ty	tau to lo gi cal
le² gis la¹ tion	per spi ca ci ty	the o lo gi cal
re ci ta tion	per ti na ci ty	re ci pro ci ty
sa cri le² g*iou*s	a tro⁵ ci ty	le² ger de ma¹in

TABLE XLIII.

Words in which h is pronounced before w, though written after it. Thus, what, when, whisper, are pronounced hwat, hwen, hwisper; that is hooat, hooen, hooisper.

wha¹le	when	whurr	whim s*ey*
whe*a*l	when*ce*	wha³rf	whin ny
whe*a*t	whet	wha⁵t	whis per
wheel	which	whirl	whis tl*e*
wheeze	whiff	whe⁹r*e*	whith er
while	whig	whey	whit lo*w*
whilst	whim	whe¹e dl*e*	whit ster
whine	whin	whi ting	whit tle
white	whip	whi tish	whim per
why	whisk	whe²r ret	
whe²lk	whist	wher ry	
whelp	whit	wheth er	
whelm	whiz	whif fl*e*	

The compounds and derivatives follow the same rule. In the following, with their compounds and derivatives, w, is silent.

who¹re	whole	who⁶	whom	whoop	whose

TABLE XLIV.

In the following, with their compounds and derivatives, x is pronounced like gz; exact is pronounced egzact, &c.

ex a^{2}ct	ex em pli fy	ex or bi tant
ex ist	ex an i mate	ex or di um
ex empt	ex as pe rate	ex a^{5}lt
ex ult	ex u^{1}de	ex ot ic
ex am ine	ex a men	ex on er rate
ex am ple	ex u ber ance	ex e^{2}rt
ex em plar	ex ha^{3}ust	ex er cent
ex ec u tor	ex hort	e^{2}x ile

In most or all other words, x is pronounced is ks, except at the beginning of Greek names, where it sounds like z.

TABLE XLV.

The history of the Creation of the World.

IN six days God made the world, and all things that are in it. He made the Sun to shine by day, and the Moon to give light by night. He made all the beasts that walk on the earth, all the birds that fly in the air, and all the fish that swim in the sea. Each herb, and plant, and tree, is the work of His hands. All things, both great and small that live and move, and breathe in this wide world, to Him do owe their birth, to Him their life. And God saw that all the things He had made were good. But as yet there was not a man to till the ground: so God made man of the dust of the earth, and breathed into him the breath of life, and gave him rule over all that He had made. And the man gave names to all the beasts of the field, the fowls of the air, and the fish of the sea. But there was not found an help meet for man; so God brought on him a deep sleep, and then took from his side a rib, of which he made a wife, and gave her to the man, and her name was Eve. And from these two came all the sons of men.

All things are known to God; though His throne of state is far on high, yet doth His eye look down upon us in this lower world, and see all the ways of the sons of men.

If we go out, He marks our steps: and when we go in, no door can shut Him from us. While we are by ourselves, He knows all our vain thoughts, and the ends we aim at. And when we talk to friend or foe, He hears our words, and views the good or harm we do to them, or to ourselves.

When we pray, He notes our zeal. All the day long He minds how we spend our time, and no dark night can hide our works from Him. If we play the cheat, He marks the fraud, and hears the least word of a false tongue.

He sees if our hearts are hard to the poor, or if by alms we help their wants: If in our breast we pine at the rich, or if we are well pleased with our own state. He knows all that we do; and be we where we will, He is sure to be with us.

TABLE XLVI.

Examples of the formation of derivatives and compound words.

EXAMPLE I.

Words in which or or er are added to denote an agent.

Prim.	Deriv.	Prim.	Deriv.
act	act-or	in-struct	in-struct-or
lead	lead-er	blas-pheme	blas-phe-mer
deal	deal-er	cor-rect	cor-rect-or
gain	gain-er	dis-pose	dis-po-ser
hate	ha-ter	op-press	op-press-or
cool	cool-er	re-deem	re-deem-er
help	help-er	dis-sent	dis-sent-er

EXAMPLE II.

Words to express females; or the feminine gender, formed from those which express males, or the masculine gender.

act-or	sor-ce-rer	proph-et-ess	em-pe-ror
bar-on	act-ress	sor-cer-ess	test-ta-tor
tu-tor	bar-on-ess	peer	seam-ster
trait-or	tu-tor-ess	priest	peer-ess
count	trait-ress	prince	priest-ess
dea-con	count-ess	po-et	prin-cess
duke	dea-con-ess	song-ster	po-et-ess
heir	duch-ess	li-on	song-stress
proph-et	heir-ess	mas-ter	li-on-ess

mis-tress	em-press	test-a-trix	seam-stress

a-dul-ter-er,	a-dul-ter-ess
em-bas-sa-dor,	em-bas-sa-dress
shep-herd,	shep-herd-ess
ben-e-fac-tor,	ben-e-fac-tress
gov-ern-or,	gov-ern-ess
mar-quis,	mar-chi-o-ness
pro-tect-or,	pro-tect-ress
ex-e-cu-tor,	ex-e-cu-trix
ad-min-is-tra-tor	ad-min-is-tra-trix

EXAMPLE III.

Words formed by ly (which is a contraction of like) used to denote a quality, or show the manner of action, or degree of quality.

bad	bad-ly	ab-struse,	ab-struse-ly
brave	brave-ly	cow-ard,	cow-ard-ly
chief	chief-ly	crook-ed,	crook-ed-ly
dark	dark-ly	ex-act,	ex-act-ly
good	good-ly	ef-fect-u-al,	ef-fect-u-al-ly
high	high-ly	ex-cess-ive,	ex-cess-ive-ly
weak	weak-ly	fa-ther,	fa-ther-ly
year	year-ly	gal-lant,	gal-lant-ly
new	new-ly	se-date,	se-date-ly

EXAMPLE IV.

Words formed by full, denoting abundance.

mer-cy	mer-ci-ful	de-ceit	de-ceit-ful
mourn	mourn-ful	re-spect	re-spect-ful
hope	hope-ful	dis-grace	dis-grace-ful
wish	wish-ful	de-light	de-light-ful
youth	youth-ful	re-venge	re-venge-ful
awe	aw-ful	dis-trust	dis-trust-ful
care	care-ful	du-ty	du-ti-ful

EXAMPLE V.

Words formed by able or ible, denoting power or ability.

com-mend	com-mend-a-ble	cure	cur-a-ble
as-sail	as-sail-a-ble	pay	pay-a-ble
re-spire	re-spi-ra-ble	sale	sale-a-ble
per-spire	per-spi-ra-ble	vend	vend-i-ble
ad-vise	ad-vi-sa-ble	test	test-a-ble
re-verse	re-vers-i-ble	taste	taste-a-ble
man-age	man-age-a-ble	tax	tax-a-ble
cred-it	cred-it-a-ble	tame	tam-a-ble
prof-it	prof-it-a-ble	rate	rat-a-ble

EXAMPLE VI.

Words formed by ness, denoting a state or condition.

good	good-ness	shrewd	shrewd-ness
great	great-ness	plain	plain-ness
rash	rash-ness	sound	sound-ness
bald	bald-ness	rough	rough-ness
hoarse	hoarse-ness	self-ish	self-ish-ness
blood-y	blood-i-ness	come-ly	come-li-ness

mis-er-a-ble,
for-mi-da-ble
gra-cious,
fa-vor-a-ble,
of-fen-sive,
mis-er-a-ble-ness
for-mi-da-ble-ness
gra-cious-ness
fa-vor-a-ble-ness
of-fen-sive-ness

EXAMPLE VII.

Words formed by ish, denoting quality or a small degree of it.

ape,	a-pish	white,	whi-tish
wasp,	wasp-ish	blue,	blu-ish
wag,	wag-gish	black,	black-ish
block,	block-ish	pur-ple,	pur-plish
sour,	sour-ish	gray,	gray-ish
sweet,	sweet-ish	clown,	clown-ish

EXAMPLE VIII.

Words formed by less, denoting destitution or absence.

art,	art-less	num-ber,	num-ber-less
grace,	grace-less	mo-tion,	mo-tion-less
shape,	shape-less	mea-sure,	mea-sure-less
need,	need-less	fa-ther,	fa-ther-less
heed,	heed-less	moth-er,	moth-er-less
care,	care-less	pray-er,	pray-er-less

EXAMPLE IX.

Words formed by al, denoting quality, and by some, noting fullness.

frac-tion,	frac-tion-al	glad,	glad-some
doc-trine,	doc-trin-al	loath,	loath-some
crime,	crim-in-al	frol-ick,	frol-ick-some
na-tion,	na-tion-al	de-light,	de-light-some

EXAMPLE X.

Words formed by ous, and ive, noting quality.

grace	gra-cious	sport	sport-ive
glo-ry	glo-ri-ous	ex-pense	ex-pen-sive
hu-mor	hu-mor-ous	con-clude	con-clu-sive
mel-o-dy	me-lo-di-ous	ex-cess	ex-ces-sive
har-mo-ny	har-mo-ni-ous	e-lect	e-lec-tive
vic-tor	vic-to-ri-ous	de-cide	de-ci-sive

EXAMPLE XI.

Words formed by age, ment, ence, and ance, denoting state, condition, or action performed, &c.

pa-rent	par-ent-age	ful-fil	ful-fil-ment
pat-ron	pat-ron-age	at-tain	at-tain-ment
per-son	per-son-age	de-pend	de-pen-dence
car-ry	car-riage	oc-cur	oc-cur-rence
mar-ry	mar-riage	re-pent	re-pen-tance
re-mit	re-mit-tance	ac-com-plish	ac-com-plish-ment
per-form	per-for-mance	com-mand	com-mand-ment

EXAMPLE XII.

Words ending in or or er and ee, the former noting the agent, and the latter the person, to whom an act is done.

les-sor´	les-see´	ap-pel-lor´	ap-pel-lee´
do´-nor	do-nee´	cog-ni-zor´	cog-ni-zee´
bail-or´	bail-ee´	in-dors´-er	in-dors-ee´
as-sign´-or	as-sign-ee´	ob-li-gor´	ob-li-gee´
pay´-or	pay-ee´	mort´-ga-ger	mort-ga-gee´

EXAMPLE XIII.

Words ending in ity, denoting power, capacity, state, &c.

in-firm	in-firm-i-ty	le-gal	le-gal-i-ty
a-ble	a-bil-i-ty	mor-tal	mor-tal-i-ty

pos-si-ble	pos-si-bil-i-ty
con-form	con-form-i-ty
chris-tian	chris-tian-i-ty
pop-u-lar	pop-u-lar-i-ty
sin-gu-lar	sin-gu-lar-i-ty
fea-si-ble	fea-si-bil-i-ty
com-pat-i-ble	com-pat-i-bil-i-ty
im-pen-e-tra-ble	im-pen-e-tra-bil-i-ty

EXAMPLE XIV.

Verbs or affirmations, formed by the terminations ize and en.

gen-er-al	gen-er-al-ize	mo-ral	mor-al-ize
le-gal	le-gal-ize	jour-nal	jour-nal-ize
tyr-an-ny	tyr-ran-nize	can-on	can-on-ize
meth-od	meth-od-ize	har-mo-ny	har-mo-nize
au-thor	au-thor-ize	strait	strait-en
bas-tard	bas-tard-ize	wide	wi´-den
sys-tem	sys-tem-ize	length	length-en
civ-il	civ-il-ize		

EXAMPLE XV.

Words in which the sense is changed by prefixing a syllable, or syllables.

ap-pear	dis-ap-pear	grow	o-ver-grow
al-low	dis-al-low	look	o-ver-look
o-bey	dis-o-bey	run	o-ver-run
o-blige	dis-o-blige	take	o-ver-take
es-teem	dis-es-teem	throw	o-ver-throw
pos-sess	dis-pos-sess	turn	o-ver-turn
ap-ply	mis-ap-ply	ad-mit	re-ad-mit
be-have	mis-be-have	as-sume	re-as-sume
in-form	mis-in-form	em-bark	re-em-bark
de-ceive	un-de-ceive	en-force	re-en-force
work	un-der-work	add	su-per-add
op-e-rate	co-op-er-ate	a-bound	su-per-a-bound
en-gage	pre-en-gage	weave	in-ter-weave
ma-ture	pre-ma-ture	see	fore-see
num-ber	out-num-ber	sight	fore-sight
run	out-run	plant	trans-plant
fee-ble,	en-fee-ble	com-pose	de-com-pose
no-ble,	en-no-ble	act	coun-ter-act

EXAMPLE XVI.

Names formed from qualities by change of termination.

long	length	deep	depth
strong	strength	wide	width

Examples of various derivatives from one root, or radical word.

Boun-ty, boun-te-ous, boun-te-ous-ly, boun-te-ous-ness, boun-ti-ful, boun-ti-ful-ly, boun-ti-ful-ness.

Beau-ty, beau-te-ous, beau-te-ous-ly, beau-te-ous-ness, beau-ti-ful, beau-ti-ful-ly, beau-ti-ful-ness, beau-ti-fy.

Art, art-ful, art-ful-ly, art-ful-ness, art-less, art-less-ly, artless-ness.

Con-form, con-form-i-ty, con-form-a-ble, con-form-a-bly, con-form-ist, con-form-a-tion, con-form-a-ble-ness.

Press, press-ure, im-press, im-press-ion, im-press-ive, im-press-ive-ly, com-press, com-press-ure, com-press-ion,

Com-press-i-ble, com-press-i-bil-i-ty, in-com-press-i-ble, in-com-press-i-bil-i-ty, de-press, de-press-ion, sup-press, sup-press-ion.

Grief, griev-ous, griev-ous-ly, griev-ance, ag-grieve.

At-tend, at-tend-ant, at-tend-ance, at-ten-tion, at-ten-tive, at-ten-tive-ly, at-ten-tive-ness.

Fa-vor, fa-vor-ite, fa-vor-a-ble, fa-vor-a-bly, fa-vor-a-ble-ness, fa-vor-it-ism, un-fa-vor-a-ble, un-fa-vor-a-bly, un-fa-vor-a-ble-ness, dis-fa-vor.

Compound Words.

ale house	cop per plate	gin ger bread
ap ple tree	day light	grand child
bed fel low	di ning room	New Ha ven
bed cham ber	Charles town	New York
bee hive	George town	ink stand
book sell er	dress ing room	ju ry man
but ter milk	drip ping pan	land tax
can dle stick	earth quake	lap dog
chain shot	el bow chair	moon shine
che ry tree	fer ry man	pa per mill
ches nut tree	fire arms	ti tle page
cop y book	fire shov el	Yale col lege

OBSERVATIONS

He seldom lives frugally, who lives by chance.

Most men are more willing to indulge in easy vices, than to practice laborious virtues.

A man may mistake the love of virtue for the practice of it; and be less a good man, than the friend of goodness.

Without frugality, none can be rich; and with it, few would be poor.

Moderation and mildness, often effect what cannot be done by force. A Persian writer finely observes, that "a gentle hand leads the elephant himself by a hair."

The most necessary part of learning is, to unlearn our errors.

Small parties make up in diligence what they want in numbers.

Some talk of subjects which they do not understand; others praise virtue, who do not practice it.

No persons are more apt to ridicule or censure others, than those who are most apt to be guilty of follies and faults.

TABLE XLVII.

Irregular words, not comprised in the foregoing tables.

Written.	Pronounced.	Written.	Pronounced.
a ny	en ny	isle	ile
bat teau	bat to	isl and	ile and
beau	bo	ma ny	men ny
beaux	boze	o cean	o shun
been	bin	says	sez
bu reau	bu ro	said	sed
bu ry	ber ry	sous	soo
bu sy	biz zy	su gar	shoo gar
co lo nel	cur nel	vis count	vi count
haut boy	ho boy	wo men	wi min

Written.	Pronounced.
ap ro pos	ap pro po
bel les let tres	bel let ter
bu si ness	biz ness
flam beau	flam bo
che vaux de frise	shev o de freeze
en ten dre	en taun der
port man teau	port man to
right eous	ri chus

The compounds and derivatives follow the same rule.

OBSERVATIONS.

Seek a virtuous man for your friend, for a vicious man can neither love long, nor be long beloved. The friendships of the wicked are conspiracies against morality and social happiness.

More persons seek to live long, though long life is not in their power; than to live well, though a good life depends on their own will.

USEFUL LESSONS.

JOHN can tell how many square rods of ground make an acre. Let me hear him. Three feet make a yard; five yards and a half make a rod or perch; forty square rods make a rood or one quarter of an acre; and one hundred and sixty square rods make an acre. One team will plow an acre in a day – sometimes more.

In solids, forty feet of round timber, or fifty feet of hewn timber, make a ton. A cord of wood contains one hundred and twenty-eight solid feet; that is, a pile four feet high, four feet wide, and eight feet long.

In cloth measure, two inches and a fifth make a nail; four nails, one quarter of a yard; thirty six inches or three feet make a yard; three quarters of a yard make an ell Flemish; and five quarters, make an English ell.

Let us examine the weights used in our own country. How are heavy goods weighed? By avoirdupois weight, in which sixteen drams make an ounce; sixteen ounces, one pound; twenty-eight pounds, one quarter of a hundred; four quarters, or one hundred and twelve pounds make a hundred; and twenty hundreds, one ton.

By this weight, are sold hay, sugar, coffee, and all heavy goods and metals, except gold and silver.

What is troy weight? It is that by which is estimated the quantity of gold and silver, jewelry, and the drugs sold by the druggist and apothecary. In troy weight, twenty-four grains make a penny weight; twenty penny weights, one ounce; and twelve ounces, one pound. These are the divisions used by the silversmith and jeweler. But the apothecary uses a different division, and in his weight, twenty grains make a scruple; three scruples one dram; eight drams, one ounce; and twelve ounces, one pound.

The dollar is one hundred cents; but the value of a pound, shilling and penny, is different in different States, and in England. English money is called Sterling. One dollar is four shillings and six pence sterling; in New England and Virginia, it is six shillings; in New York and North Carolina, it is eight shillings; in New Jersey, Pennsylvania, Delaware and Maryland, it is seven shillings and six pence; in South Carolina and Georgia, it is four shillings and eight pence. But these differences give great trouble, and will soon be laid aside as useless. All money will be reckoned in dollars and cents.

Inhabitants of the United States according to the census of 1800.

New Hampshire	183, 000
Massachusetts	575, 000
Rhode Island	70, 000
Connecticut	251, 000
Vermont	154, 000
New York	586, 000
New Jersey	211, 000
Pennsylvania	604, 000
Delaware	64, 000
Maryland	322, 000
Virginia	886, 000
North Carolina	478, 000
South Carolina	345, 000
Georgia	162, 000
Kentucky	220, 000
Tennessee	137, 000

OBSERVATIONS AND MAXIMS

THE path of duty, is always the path of safety.

Be very cautious in believing ill of your neighbor; but more cautious in reporting it.

It requires but little discernment to discover the imperfections of others; but much humility to acknowledge our own.

Many evils incident to human life are unavoidable; but no man is vicious, except by his own choice.

Avoid vicious company, where the good are often made bad, and the bad worse. If the good ever associate with evil men, it should be for the same reason as a physician visits the sick, – not to catch the disease, but to cure it.

Some people are lost for want of good advice but more for want of giving heed to it.

TABLE XLVIII.

The most usual Names of Men, accented.

Aa´ ron	Ed´ mund	Ich´ a bod
A´ bel	Ed´ ward	
A´ bram	Ed´ win	Ja´ bez
Ad´ am	Ed´ gar	Ja´ cob
Al´ bert	Eg´ bert	James
Al´ len	E le a´ zar	Jef´ frey
Al ex an´ der	El´ dad	Job
Al´ fred	E´ li	Jo´ el
Am´ brose	E li´ as	John
A´ mos	E li´ zur	Jo´ nas
An´ drew	E li´ sha	Jo´ seph
An´ tho ny	E liph´ a let	Jo si´ ah
Ar´ chi bald	E´ noch	Josh´ u a
Ar´ nold	E´ phraim	Jude
Ar´ thur	E ze´ ki el	Jus tus
Au´ stin	E ras´ tus	Jer e mi´ ah
A´ sa hel	Ez´ ra	Jon´ a than
A´ saph	Eb e ne´ zer	Ja´ red
A´ sa		Jes´ se
Ash´ er	Fran´ cis	
	Fred´ er ic	Leon´ ard
Bar´ na bas		Lew´ is
Ben´ ja min	Ga´ briel	Lu´ cius
Ben´ net	George	Luke
Ber´ nard	Gid´ e on	Lem´ u el
Brad´ ford	Gil´ bert	Le´ vi
	Giles	Lu´ ther
Ca´ leb	God´ frey	
Charles	Greg´ o ry	Mark
Chris´ to pher		Mar´ tin
Cor ne´ li us	Hen´ ry	Mat´ thew
Clark	Hugh	Mi´ chael
Cyp´ ri an	Ho ra´ tio	Miles
	Hor´ ace	Mor´ gan
Dan´ iel	Hez e ki´ ah	Mo´ ses
Da´ vid		Me´ dad
Den´ nis	I´ saac	
	Is´ rael	Na´ than

Na than´ iel
Ne he mi´ ah
Nich´ o las
Nor´ man

O ba di´ ah
Ol´ i ver

Pe´ ter
Paul
Phil´ ip
Phin´ e as

Ralph
Reu´ ben

Rich´ ard
Rob´ ert
Rog´ er
Ru´ fus

Sam´ u el
Seth
Sil ves´ ter
Sim´ e on
Si´ mon
Sol´ o mon
Ste´ phen
Si´ las

The´ o dore

The oph´ i lus
Thom´ as
Tim´ o thy
Ti´ tus

U ri´ ah

Val´ en tine
Vin´ cent

Wal´ ter
Will´ iam

Za´ doc
Zech a ri´ ah

Names of Women

Ab´ i gail
A´ my
Ann
An´ na
An´ nis
A me´ lia

Bridg´ et
Be lin´ da

Car´ o line
Cla ris´ sa
Ce´ li a

Deb´ o rah
Di´ nah
Dor´ cas
Dor´ o thy
De´ li a

El´ ea nor
E li´ za
E liz´ a beth
Em´ ma

Em´ i ly
Es´ ther
Eu´ nice
E mil´ ia

Faith
Flo´ ra
Fran´ ces

Grace

Han´ nah
Har´ ri et
Hel´ en
Hen ri et´ ta
Hes´ ter
Hul´ dah

Is´ a bel

Jane
Je mi´ ma
Jen´ net
Ju´ li a

Ju li an´

Kath´ a rine

Love
Lu´ cy
Lyd´ ia
Lu cre´ tia
Lu cin´ da

Ma´ bel
Mar´ ga ret
Mar´ tha
Ma´ ry
Ma ri´ a

Nan´ cy

Pa´ tience
Pen el´ o pe
Phe´ be
Phil´ lis
Pris cil´ la
Pru´ dence

Ra´ chel
Re bec´ ca
Ruth
Rose

Sa´ rah
So phi´ a
Sal´ ly
Su san´ nah

Su´ san

Tem´ per ance

Ur su´ la

Derivatives from Names.

Am´ mon   Am´ mon ite
Ca´ naan   Ca´ naan ite
E´ phraim   E´ phraim ite
Mo´ ab   Mo´ ab ite
Cal´ vin   Cal´ vin ist
Lu´ ther   Lu´ ther an
Is´ rael   Is´ rael ite
Rome   Ro´ man
Cor´ inth   Cor inth´ i an
Ath´ ens   Ath e´ ni an
Ha´ gar   Ha´ gar enes
Ga la´ tia   Ga la´ tians
Sa ma´ ri a   Sa mar´ i tans
Am´ a lek   Am´ a ´lek ite
E´ dom   E´ dom ite
Beth´ le hem   Beth´ le hem ite
Lon´ don   Lon´ don er
Par´ is   Pa ris´ ian
Ben´ ja min   Ben´ ja min ite
Reu´ ben   Reu´ ben ite
Jew   Jew´ ish
New´ ton   New to´ ni an
Al ex an´ dri a   Al ex an´ dri an
Ci´ ce ro   Ci´ ce ro´ ni an
Co per´ nic us   Co per´ ni can
Ep i cu´ rus   Ep i cu´ re an
Ga´ li lee   Gal li le´ an
Ma hom´ et   Ma hom´ e tan
Sad du cee´   Sad du ce´ an
Phar´ i see   Phar i sa´ ic
Pla´ to   Pla ton´ ic
     Pla´ to nist
Chal de´ a   Chal de´ an
Cy re´ ne   Cy re´ ni an

Gil´ e ad	Gil´ e ad ite
Her´ od	He ro´ di ans
Ish´ ma el,	Ish´ ma el ite
Mid´ i an,	Mid´ i an ite
Tyre	Tyr´ i a

TABLE XLIX.

Names of the principal Countries on the Eastern Continent, the adjective belonging to each, the name of the People, and the chief Town or City – accented.

Country.	Adjective.	People.	Chief Cities.
A´ sia,	A siat´ ic	A siat´ ics	
Af´ ri ca	Af´ ri can	Af´ ri cans	
Aus´ tri a	Aus´ tri an	Aus´ tri ans	Vi en´ na
A ra´ bi a	Ar´ a bic	A ra´ bi ans	Mec´ ca
	A ra´ bi an	or A´ rabs	
Al gie´rs	Al ge ri´ne	Al ge rines	Al gi´ ers
Brit´ ain	Brit´ ish	Brit´ ons	
Eng´ land	Eng´ lish	Eng´ lish	Lon´ don
Scot´ land	Scotch	Scots	Ed´ in burgh
		I´ rish or	
I´re land	I´ rish	I´ rish men	Dub´ lin
Hi ber´ ni a	Hi ber´ ni an	Hi ber´ ni ans	
Wales	Welch	Welch´ men	
Bo he´ mi a	Bo he´ mi an	Bo he´ mi ans	Prague
	Chi ne´ se		
Chi´ na	Chi´ na	Chi ne´ se	Pe´ king
Cor´ si ca	Cor´ si can	Cor´ si cans	Bas´ tia
Den´ mark	Da´ nish	Danes	Co pen ha´ gen
E´ gypt	E gyp´ tian	E gyp´ tians	Cai´ ro or
			Cai ra
Eu´ rope	Eu ro pe´ an	Eu ro pe´ ans	
Flan´ ders	Flem´ ish	Flem´ ings	Brus´ sels
Bel´ gi um	Bel´ gi an	Bel´ gi ans	Brus´ sels
France	French	French	Par´ is
	Gal´ lic, or	or	
Gaul	Gal´ li can	Gauls	Par´ is
Fran co´ ni a	Fran co´ ni an	Fran co´ ni ans	Wurts´ burg
Ger´ ma ny	Ger´ man or	Ger´ mans	Vi en´ na
	Ger man´ ic		

Ba va´ ri a	Ba va´ ri an	Ba va´ ri ans	Mu´ nich
Gen´ o a	Gen o e´se	Gen o e´se	Gen´ o a
Li gu´ ri a	Li gu´ ri an	Li gu´ ri ans	Gen´ o a
Greece	Gre´ cian	Greeks	Ath´ ens
Hol´ land	Dutch	Dutch or	Am´ ster dam
		Hol´ lan ders	Hague
Ba ta´ vi a	Ba ta´ vi an	Ba ta´ vi ans	Am´ ster dam
			Hague
			Pres´ burg, or
Hun´ ga ry	Hun ga´ ri an	Hun ga´ ri ans	Bu´ da
It´ a ly	I tal´ ian, or	I tal´ i ans	Rome
	I tal´ ic		
Ice´ land	Ice land´ ic	I´ce land ers	
In´ di a	In´ di an	In´ di an	Del´ hi
	Hin´ du	Hin´ dus	Cal cut´ ta
	Hin´ doo	Hin´ doos	
In du´ stan	Gen´ too	Gen´ toos	Ma dras
Ja pan´	Jap an e´se	Jap an e´se	
Mi lan e´se	Mi lan e´se	Mi lan e´se	Mi lan´
Mo roc´ co	Moor´ ish	Moors	Fez
Na´ ples	Ne a pol´ i tan,	Ne a pol´ i tans	Na´ ples
Nor´ way	Nor we´ gi an	Nor we´ gi ans	Ber´ gen
Per´ sia	Per´ sian	Per´ sians	Is pa han´
Pied mont´	Pied mon te´ se	Pied mon te´ se	Turin
Po´ land	Po´ lish	Po´ land ers	War´ saw
		or Poles	
Por´ tu gal	Por´ tu guese	Por´ tu guese	Lis´ bon
Prus´ sia	Prus´ sian	Prus´ sians	Ber´ lin
Rus´ sia	Rus´ sian	Rus´ sians	Pe´ ters burg
Si´ ci ly	Si cil´ i an	Si cil´ i ans	Pa ler´ mo
Spain	Span´ ish	Span´ iards	Ma drid´
Sar din´ i a	Sar din´ i an	Sar din´ i ans	Cag li a´ ri
Swe´ den	Swe´ dish	Swedes	Stock´ holm
			Bern´ or
Swit´ zer land	Swiss	Swiss	Basle
Sax´ o ny	Sax´ on	Sax´ ons	Dres´ den
Swa´ bi a	Swa´ bi an	Swa´ bi ans	Augs´ burg
Tur´ key	Turk´ ish	Turks	Con´ stan ti no´ ple
Tar´ ta ry	Tar´ tar	Tar´ tars	To bol´ ski
	Tar ta´ ri an		Thi´ bet
Tu nis	Tu nis´ ian	Tu nis´ ians	Tu´ nis
Tus´ ca ny	Tus´ cans	Tus´ cans	Flor´ ence

Si´ am	Si am e´se	Si am e´se	Si am´
Ton´ quin	Ton quin e´se	Ton quin e´se	Tong too´
Ven´ ice	Ve ne´ tian	Ve ne´ tians	Ven´ ice

In America

States.	Chief Towns.	People.
America	American	Amer´ i cans
States.	**Chief Towns.**	**People.**
New Hamp´ shire	Po´rts mouth	
Maine, in	Po´rt land	
Mas sa chu´ setts	Bos´ ton	Bos to´ ni ans
Ver mont´	Ben´ ning ton	
	Rut´ land &	Ver mont´ ers
	Wind´ sor	
Rhode I´s land	Prov´ i dence &	Rhode I´s land ers
	New´ port	
Con nec´ ti cut	Hart´ ford	
	New Ha´ ven &	
	New Lon´ don	
New York	New York &	New York´ ers
	Al´ ba ny	
New Jer´ sey	Tren´ ton	
	E liz´ a beth town	
Penn syl va´ ni a	Prince´ ton &	Penn syl va´ ni ans
	New´ ark	
Del´ a ware	Phil a del´ phi a &	
	Lan´ cas ter	
Ma´ ry land	Wil´ ming ton &	Ma´ ry land ers
	Do´ ver	
	Bal´ ti more &	
	An nap´ o lis	Vir gin´ i ans
Vir gin´ i a	Rich´ mond	
	Al ex an´ dri a &	
	Nor´ folk	
North Car o li´ na	New´ bern	Car o lin´ i ans
	Wil´ ming ton &	
	E´ den ton	
South Car o li´ na	Charles´ ton &	Car o lin´ i ans
	Co lum´ bi a	
Ge or´ gi a	Sa van´ na &	Ge or´ gi ans
	Au gus´ ta	
Ken tuck´ y	Lex´ ing ton	Ken tuck´ i ans
Ten nes see´	Nash´ ville	Ten nes se´ ans
O hi´ o	Chil li co´ tha	
Lou is ian´ a	New Or´ leans	Lou is ia´ ni ans

British, Spanish and Portuguese America

Provinces.	Chief Towns.	People.
Can´ a da	Que bec´	Ca na´ di ans
New Bruns´ wick	St. Johns	
No´ va Sco´ tia	Hal´ i fax	
E. Flor´ i da	Au gus ti´ne	
W. Flor´ i da	Pen sa co´ la	
Mex´ i co	Mex´ i co	Mex´ i cans
Chi´ le	St. Ja´ go	Chil´ i ans
Pe ru´	Li´ ma	Pe ru´ vi ans
Qui´ to	Qui´ to	
Par a gua´y	Buen´ os ayres	
Bra zil´	St. Sal va do´re	Bra zil´ i ans

TABLE L.

Chief Rivers on the Eastern Continent

IN EUROPE.

Dan´ ube	Loire	Scheldt*
Don or	Med´ way	Sev´ ern
Ta na´ is	Maes	Shan´ non
Drave	Mo sell´e	Seine
Du´ ro	Nie´ per, or	Soane
Dwi´ na	Bo rist´ he nes	Tay
E´ bro	Nie´ men	Ta´ gus
Elbe	Nie´ ster	Thames
Eu ro´ tas	O´ der	Ti´ ber
Ga ro´nne	Pe ne´ us	Vis´ tu la
Gua´ del quiv ier	Po	We´ ser
Gua di an´ a	Rhone	Wol´ ga, or
Hum´ ber	Rhine	Vol´ ga

*Pronounced Shelt.

IN AFRICA.

Ba gra´ da, or	Sen e gal´	Or´ ange
Me ger´ da	Ni´ ger, or	Gau rit´z
Nile	Jol i ba´	

IN ASIA.

A rax´ es
A´ va
Cu ban´
Eu phra´ tes
Gan´ ges
Ha´ lys
In´ dus, or Sind

Ir tis
Jen i see´
Kur, or
Cy´ rus
Me an´ der
Me non´
Me con´

O´ by
Ox´ us
Pe gu´
Rha
Ti´ gris
Yel low, or
Ho ang´ he

Oceans.

At lan´ tic

Pa cif´ ic

In´ di an

Seas.

Bal´ tic
Cas´ pi an

Eu´x ine
Med i ter ra´ ne an

Me o´ tis, or
A´ zoph

Bays and Gulfs.

A dri at´ ic
Baf´ fins
Bis´ cay
Both´ ni a

Cal i for´ ni a
Ches´ o peak
Cha leu´r
Fin´ land

Fun´ dy
Hud´ sons
Mex´ i co
Ri ga´

Lakes in Europe and Asia.

As phal´ tis
Bai´ kal
Co´ mo
Con stance´

Ge ne´ va
Gar´ da
Is´ co
La do´ ga

Lu ga´ na
Mag gi o´re
O ne´ ga
Wi nan´

Mountains in Europe, Africa and Asia.

Alps
Ap´ pe nines
Ar´ ra rat
At´ las
Ce vennes´
Cau´ ca sus

Car´ mel
Et´ na
Heck´ la
Ho´ reb
I´ da

Ju´ ra
Py re nee´s
Si´ nai
Tau´ rus
Ve su´ vi us´

Mountains in America.

An´ des, or
Cor dil´ ler as

Al le ga´ ny
Cats´ kill

Kit ta kin´ ny
O le roy´

Chief Rivers in America.

Am´ a zon, or
Mar´ a non
Al´ ba ny
Ap a lach´ y
Ap´ a lach´ i co´ la
Ar´ kan saw
Al ta ma haw´
An dros cog´ gin
Buf´ fa lo
Cum´ ber land
Chat ta ho´ chy
Clar´ en don, or
Cape Fear
Chow an´
Con nec´ ti cut
Co lum´ bi a, or
Ta co´ chy
Chau di e´re
Del´ a ware
E dis´ to
Elk
Flint
Hack´ en sac
Hou sa ton´ uc
Hock hock´ ing
Hud´ son
Il li nois´
I´ ro quois, or
St. Law´ rence

Ja ne´ i ro
James, or
Pow hat tan´
Kan ha´ way
Ken tuc´ ky
Ken ne bec´
Lick´ ing
La moil´
Mis si sip´ pi
Mis sou´ ri
Musk ing´ um
Mi am´ i
Mo bill´
Mis sisk´ o
Mer´ ri mae
Moose
Ma ken´ zie
Nuse
Nel´ son
O ro no´ ke
O hi´ o
O gee´ chy
On´ ion
Par a gua´y, or
Plate
Pa to´ mac
Pearl
Pas cat´ a way
Pe nob´ scot

Pas sa´ ic
Pe dee´
Roan o´ke
Rap pa han´ noc
Rar´ i ton
Sa van´ na
San tee´
Sa lu´ da
Sa til´ la
Sus que han´ na
Schu´yl kill
Sci o´ ta
Sau´ co
Scoo´ duc
St. John
St. Ma´ ry
Sev´ ern
Sas ka shaw´ in
So rell´
Sag u nau´
Ten nes see´
Tu´ gu lo
Tom big´ by
Un´ ji ga
U ta was´
Wat ter ee´
Wau´ bosh
York
Ya zoo´

Lakes in America.

Cay u´ ga
Can a dar´ qua
Cham pla´in

E´ rie
George
Hu´ ron

Mich´ i gan
Moose´ head
Mem fre ma´ gog

Ot se´ go	Sen´ e ka	Win´ ni pis i o´ gy
O nei´ da	Su pe´ ri or	Win´ ni pic
On ta´ ri o	Tez cu´ co	Wa´ que fa no´ ga or
On an da´ go	Um´ ba gog	O´ ka fa no´ ke

TABLE LI.

Names of Cities, Towns, Counties, Rivers, Mountains, Lakes, Islands, Bays, &c. in America.

The following have the accent on the first syllable.

A

Ab´ er corn	Ar row sike	
Ab ing don	Ar u ba	
Ab ing ton	Ash burn ham	Barn sted
Ab se con	Ash by	Bar re
Ac ton	Ash field	Bar rets ton
Ad ams	Ash ford	Bar ring ton
Ac worth	Ash ton	Bart let
Al ba ny	Ash we lot	Bar ton
Al bi on	As sa bet	Bart
Al ford	A thol	Bath
Al lens town	At kin son	Bat ten kill
All burg	At tle bo rough	Bea ver
Al lo way	Av a lon	Beau fort
All saints	A ve ril	Beck et
Alms bu ry	Av on	Bed ford
Al stead	Ayers ton	Bed min ster
Am boy		Beek man
Am e lins	**B**	Belch er
Ame well	Bairds town	Bel fast
Am herst	Ba kers field	Bel grade
Am ster dam	Ba kers town	Bel ling ham
An do ver	Ball town	Ben ning ton
An ge lo	Bal ti more	Ben e dict
An ge los	Ban gor	Ben son
An trim	Bar ba ra	Ber gen
An vill	Bar nard	Berk ley
Aq ue fort	Bar ne velt	Berk shire
Arm strong	Bar ne gat	Ber lin
Ar ling ton	Bar net	Ber nards town
	Barn sta ble	Bern

Ber wick
Beth a ny
Beth el
Beth le hem
Bev er ly
Bil lings port
Bir ming ham
Black stone
Bla den
Bla dens burg
Blan ca
Blan co
Bland ford
Bled soe
Blen heim
Block ley
Bloom field
Bloom ing dale
Blount
Blounts ville
Blue hill
Bol in broke
Bol ton
Bom bay
Bom ba zin
Bon a ven ture
Bon a vis ta
Bon ham town
Boone ton
Boons bo rough
Bop quam
Bor den town
Bot e tourt
Bot tle hill
Bound brook
Bour bon
Bow doin
Bow doin ham
Bow ling green
Box bo rough
Box ford
Boyl ston
Boz rah

Brad ford
Brain tree
Bran don
Bran dy wine
Bran ford
Brat tle bo rough
Breck nock
Brent wood
Bre ton
Bridge town
Bridge wa ter
Bridge port
Brid port
Brim field
Bris tol
Brom ley
Brook field
Brook lyn
Broth er ton
Brough ton
Brown field
Brun ners town
Browns ville
Bruns wick
Bru tus
Buck land
Buc kles town
Bucks town
Buck town
Bull skin
Burke
Bur ling ton
Bur ton
Bush town
Bush wick
Bus tard
But ler
But ter field
But ter hill
Bux ton
Buz zards bay
By ber ry
Bye field

By ram

C
Cab ot
Ca diz
Cal ais
Cal ders burg
Cal la o
Cal vert
Cam bridge
Cam den
Camp bell
Cam po bel lo
Camp ton
Ca naan
Can dia
Can ons burg
Can so
Can ter bu ry
Can ton
Car di gan
Car ibs
Car los
Car mel
Car mel o
Car ne ro
Carns ville
Car o line
Car ter
Car ter et
Car ters ville
Car ver
Cas co
Cas tle ton
Cas tel town
Cas well
Ca to
Cats kill
Cav en dish
Cay mans
Ce cil
Cen ter
Cham bers burg

Chap el hill
Chance ford
Charles ton
Charles town
Charle ton
Char lotte
Char lottes ville
Chat ham
Chelms ford
Chel sea
Chel ten ham
Chesh ire
Ches ter
Ches ter field
Ches ter town
Chick o py
Chi ches ter
Chip pe ways
Chil mark
Chitt en den
Choc taws
Chris tians burg
Chris tian sted
Chris to phers
Church town
Ci ce ro
Clar en don
Clarks burg
Clarkes town
Clarkes ville
Clav er ack
Clin ton
Clinch
Clos ter
Cob ham
Co bles hill
Cock burne
Cock er mouth
Coey mans
Cokes bu ry
Col ches ter
Cole brook
Con cord

Con way
Coots town
Cor inth
Cor nish
Corn wall
Cort landt
Cov en try
Cow pens
Cox hall
Crab or chard
Cran ber ry
Cra ney
Crans ton
Cra ven
Craw ford
Cross wicks
Cro ton
Crown point
Croy den
Cul pep per
Cum ber land
Cum ming ton
Cus co
Cush e tunk
Cush ing
Cus sens
Cus si tah

D
Dal ton
Dan bu ry
Dan by
Dan vers
Dan ville
Dar by
Dar i en
Dar ling ton
Dart mouth
Dau phin
Da vid son
Ded ham
Deer field
Deer ing

Den nis
Den ton
Dept ford
Der by
Der ry
Der ry field
Dig by
Digh ton
Dis mal
Don ne gal
Dor ches ter
Dor lach
Dor set
Doug las
Down ings
Dra cut
Dres den
Dro more
Drum mond
Dry den
Duck creek
Duck trap
Dud ley
Dum mer
Dum mers town
Dun cans burg
Dun der burg
Dun sta ble
Dur ham
Duch ess
Dux bo rough
Dux bu ry
Dy ber ry

E
Eas ter ton
East ham
East on
East town
Ea ton
Ea ton town
E den
Edes ton

Ed gar ton
Edge comb
Edge field
Edge mont
Ef fing ham
Egg har bor
Eg mont
Eg re mont
El bert
El bert son
Elk
Elk horn
Elk ridge
Elk ton
El ling ton
El lis
El more
Em mits burg
En field
En glish town
E no
E nos burg
Ep ping
Ep som
Er rol
Er vin
Es qui maux
Es sex
Est her town
Eus tace
Ev ans ham
Eves ham
Ex e ter

F
Fa bi us
Fair fax
Fair field
Fair lee
Falk land
Fal mouth
Fals ing ton
Fan net

Fa quier
Far ming ton
Fay ette ville
Fays town
Fed er als burg
Fells point
Fer ris burg
Fin cas tle
Find ley
Fish ers field
Fish kill
Fitch burg
Flat land
Flem ing ton
Fletch er
Flints ton
Flow er town
Floyd
Flush ing
Fol low field
For est er ton
Fram ing ham
Fran ces town
Fran cis burg
Fran cois
Frank fort
Frank lin
Franks town
Fred e ri ca
Fred e rick
Fred e ricks burg
Fred e ricks town
Free hold
Free port
Free town
Fried burg
Fried land
Fried en stadt
Fry burg
Frow sack

G
Gal en

Gal lo way
Gal way
Gard ner
Gas pee
Gates
Gay head
George town
Ger man town
Ger ma ny
Ger ry
Get tys burg
Gill
Gil lo ri
Gil man town
Gil son
Glas gow
Glas ten bu ry
Glouces ter
Glov er
Glynn
Goffs town
Golds burg
Gol phing ton
Gooch land
Gor ham
Go shen
Gos port
Go tham
Graf ton
Grain ger
Gren a dines
Gran ville
Gray
Green burg
Green cas tle
Green field
Green land
Greens burg
Greens ville
Green wich
Green wood
Gregs town
Gro ton

Gry son
Guil ford
Gur net
Guys burg

H
Hack ets town
Had dam
Had don field
Had ley
Ha gars town
Hal lam
Hal low el
Ham den
Ham burg
Ham il ton
Ham mels town
Hamp shire
Hamp sted
Hamp ton
Han cock
Han nahs town
Han ni bal
Han o ver
Har din
Hard wick
Har dy
Har dys town
Har ford
Har lem
Har mo ny
Har mar
Har pers field
Har ple
Harps well
Har ring ton
Har ris burg
Har ri son
Har rods burg
Hart ford
Hart land
Har vard
Har wich

Har win ton
Hat burg
Hat field
Hat chy
Hat te ras
Hav er ford
Ha ver hill
Hav er straw
Haw
Hawke
Haw kins
Haw ley
Hay cock
Heath
He bron
Hec tor
Hei dle berg
Hell gate
Hem lock
Hemp field
Hen ni ker
Hen ri co
Hen ry
Her ke mer
Hert ford
Hi ats town
Hick mans
High gate
High land
Hills dale
Hills burg
Hill town
Hines burg
Hing ham
Hins dale
Hi ram
Hit ton
Ho bok
Hol den
Hol der ness
Hol land
Hol lis
Hol lis ton

Hols ton
Ho mer
Hon ey goe
Hooks town
Hoo sac
Hop kin ton
Hop kins
Hope well
Horn town
Horse neck
Hors ham
Hor ton
Ho sac
Hub bard ton
Hub ber ton
Hughs burg
Hum mels town
Hun ger ford
Hun ter don
Hun ters town
Hun ting don
Hunt ing ton
Hunts burg
Hunts ville
Hur ley
Hydes park

I
Ib ber ville
In gra ham
In ver ness
Ips wich
I ras burg
Ire dell
Ir vin
Isles burg
I slip

J
Jack son
Jack sons burg
Jaf frey
Ja go

James
James town
Jay
Jef fer son
Jek yl
Jenk in town
Jer e mie
Jer i ce
Jer sey
Johns bu ry
John son
John son burg
Johns town
Johns ton
Jones
Jones burg
Jop pa
Jore
Ju dith
Ju lian
Ju li et
Ju ni us

K
Keene
Kel lys burg
Ken net
Ken no mic
Ken sing ton
Kent
Kep lers
Ker shaw
Kick a muit
Kil ling ly
Kil ling ton
Kil ling worth
Kim bec
King less
Kings bu ry
Kings ton
King wood
Kit te ry
Knowl ton

Knox
Knoul ton
Knox ville
Kort right

L
Lab ra dor
Lam pe ter
Lam prey
Lan cas ter
Lang don
Lanes bo rough
Lan sing burg
Law rence
Lau rens
Lea cock
Lees burg
Leb a non
Leeds
Le high
Leices ter
Lem ing ton
Lemps ter
Len ox
Le o gane
Leom in ster
Le on
Leon ards town
Lev er ett
Le vi
Lew is
Lew is burg
Lew is town
Lex ing ton
Ley don
Lib er ty
Lich te nau
Lick ing
Lim er ick
Lime stone
Lin coln
Lin coln town
Lind ley

Litch field
Lit tle burg
Lit tle ton
Liv er more
Liv er pool
Liv ing ston
Locke
Lock arts burg
Lo gan
Logs town
Lon don der ry
Lon don grove
Look out
Lou don
Loch a bar
Lou is ville
Lou is town
Loy al soc
Lud low
Lum ber ton
Lu nen burg
Lur gan
Lut ter lock
Ly man
Lyme
Lynch burg
Lynde burg
Lyn den
Lynn
Lynn field
Ly ons
Lys tra

M
Mac o keth
Mac o pin
Mad bu ry
Mad i son
Maid stone
Maine
Make field
Mal a bar
Mal den

Mar o nec

Man ca

Man chac

Man ches ter

Man heim

Man li us

Man ning ton

Man or

Man sel

Mans field

Mar ble ton

Mar ga rets ville

Mar got

Marl bo rough

Mar low

Mar ple

Marsh field

Mar tic

Mar tin

Mar tins burg

Mar tins ville

Mas co my

Ma son

Mas sac

Mas ti gon

Mat thews

May field

Mead ville

Meck len burg

Med field

Med ford

Med way

Mend ham

Men don

Mer cer

Mer cers burg

Mer e dith

Mer i meg

Mer i on

Me ro

Mes sers burg

Mid dle bo rough

Mid dle bu ry

Mid dle field

Mid dle hook

Mid dle berg

Mid dle burg

Mid dle sex

Mid dle ton

Mid dle town

Mid way

Miff lin

Mil ford

Mil field

Mil lers town

Mill stone

Mill town

Mil ton

Min gun

Min goes

Min i sink

Mis tic

Mo hawk

Monk ton

Mon mouth

Mon son

Mon ta gue

Mont mo rin

Moore

Moore field

Moose head

More land

More

Mor gan

Mor gan town

Mor ris town

Mor ris ville

Moul ton berg

Mul li cus

Mun cy

Mur frees burg

My ers town

N

Nan je my

Nan ti coke

Nan ti mill

Nash

Nash u a

Nas sau

Natch es

Na tick

Nau ga tuc

Nave sink

Naz a reth

Ned dick

Need ham

Nel son

Nes co pec

Nesh a noc

Nev er sink

New ark

New burg

New bu ry

New bu ry port

New found land

New ing ton

New lin

New mar ket

New ton

New town

Nit ta ny

Nix on ton

No ble burg

None such

Noot ka

Nor ridge woe

Nor ri ton

North bo rough

North bridge

North field

North port

North wood

Nor ton

Nor walk

Nor way

Nor wich

Not ta way

Not ting ham

Nox an

O
Oak ham
O bed
O bi on
O cri coc
O gle thorp
O hi ope
Old town
Ons low
Or ange
Or ange burg
Or ange town
Or ford
Or le ans
Or ring ton
Or wel
Os na burg
Os si py
Os ti co
O tis field
Ot ta was
Ot ter creek
Ou li out
Ov id
Ox ford

P
Pack ers field
Pac o let
Pal a tine
Palm er
Pam ti co
Pan ton
Pa ri a
Par is
Pax tang
Par sons field
Par tridge field
Pat ter son
Pau ca tuc
Paw ling

Pauls burg
Paw let
Pax ton
Peach am
Pea cock
Pearl
Peeks kill
Pel ham
Pel i can
Pem i gon
Pem broke
Pen dle ton
Pen guin
Pen ning ton
Penns burg
Penns bu ry
Pep in
Pep per el
Pep per el burg
Pe quot
Per ki o my
Per lic an
Per son
Pe ter bo rough
Pe ters burg
Pe ters ham
Pey tons burg
Phil ip
Phil ips burg
Pick ers ville
Pic o let
Pi geon
Pike land
Pi lot town
Pinck ney
Pinck ney ville
Pis to let
Pitt
Pitts burg
Pitts field
Pitts ford
Pitts town
Plain field

Plais tow
Platts burg
Plum sted
Plym outh
Plymp ton
Po land
Pom fret
Pomp ton
Pomp ey
Pop lin
Por pess
Por ter field
Port land
Ports mouth
Pot ters
Pot ters town
Potts grove
Poult ney
Pow nal
Pow nal burg
Prai ry
Pres cot
Pres ton
Pros pect
Prov ince
Prov ince town
Pru dence
Pur rys burg
Put ney

Q
Qua ker town
Quee chy
Queens bu ry
Queens town
Quib ble town
Quin e paug
Quin cy
Quin e paug

R
Ra by
Rad nor

Ra leigh
Ran dolph
Ran dom
Ra pha el
Raph oc
Raw don
Rah way
Ray mond
Rayn ham
Rays town
Read field
Read ing
Red ding
Read ing town
Reeds burg
Reel foot
Reams town
Reis ters town
Rens se laer
Rens se laer wick
Rhine beck
Rich field
Rich mond
Ridge field
Rid ley
Rindge
Rin gos town
Rob ert son
Rob e son
Roch es ter
Rock bridge
Rock fish
Rock ford
Rock hill
Rock ing ham
Ro gers ville
Rom ney
Rom o pac
Rom u lus
Rose way
Ros sig nol
Rot ter dam
Rowe

Row ley
Rox burg
Rox bu ry
Roy al ton
Roy als ton
Rum ney
Ru pert
Rus sel
Ruth er ford
Ruths burg
Rye
Rye gate

S

Sa lem
Sack ville
Sad bu ry
Sau ga tuc
Sal ford
Salis bu ry
Sam burg
Samp town
Samp son
San born ton
San co ty
Sand gate
San dis field
San down
Sand wick
San dy hook
San dys ton
Sand ford
San ger field
San ta cruse
Sas sa fras
Sau con
Sau kies
Sav age
Say brook
Scar bo rough
Scars dale
Sho dack
Shen brun

Scoo duc
Schuy ler
Scip i o
Scit u ate
Scriv en
Scroon
Sea brook
Sears burg
Sedg wick
See konk
Se gum
Sen e ka
Sev ern
Se vi er
Shafts bu ry
Sham mo ny
Sham o kin
Shap liegh
Sha ron
Sharks town
Sharps burg
Shaw ny
Shaw nees
Sheep scut
Shef field
Shel burn
Shel by
Shen an do ah
Shep herds field
Shep herds town
Sher burn
Ship pands town
Ship pens burg
Shir ley
Shong um
Shore ham
Shrews bu ry
Shutes bu ry
Sid ney
Sims bu ry
Sing sing
Sin i ca
Sin pink

Skenes burg
Skup per nong
Skip ton
Sku tock
Slab town
Smith field
Smith town
Smith ville
Smyr na
Snow hill
Snow town
So dus
Sole bu ry
So lon
Som ers
Som er set
Som ers worth
Son go
South bo rough
South bu ry
South field
South ing ton
South wark
South wick
Span ish town
Spar ta
Spar tan burg
Spen cer
Spots wood
Spring field
Spur wing
Squam
Staats burg
Staf ford
Stam ford
Stand ish
Stan ford
Stan wix
Starks burg
States burg
Staun ton
Ster ling
Steu ben

Ste vens
Ste vens burg
Ste ven town
Ste phen town
Still wa ter
Stock bridge
Stock port
Stod dard
Stokes
Stone ham
Ston ing ton
Sto no
Stou e nuck
Stough ton
Stow
Straf ford
Stras burg
Strat ford
Strat ham
Strat ton
Stums town
Stur bridge
Styx
Steu ben ville
Stis sick
Sud bu ry
Suf field
Suf folk
Suf frage
Sul li van
Su mans town
Sum ner
Sun a py
Sun bu ry
Sun cook
Sun der land
Sur ry
Sus sex
Sut ton
Swams cot
Swans burg
Swan sey
Swan ton

Swan town
Swedes burg
Syd ney

T
Tal bot
Tam ma ny
Tam worth
Ta ney town
Ten saw
Tar bo rough
Tar ry town
Taun ton
Teach es
Tel li co
Tem ple
Tem ple ton
Tewks bu ry
Thames
Thet ford
Thom as
Thom as town
Thomp son
Thorn bu ry
Thorn ton
Thur man
Tin i cum
Tin mouth
Tis bu ry
Tiz on
Tiv er ton
Tol land
Tomp son town
Tops field
Tops ham
Tor but
Tor ring ton
Tot te ry
Tow er hill
Towns end
Trap
Trap town
Trent

Tren ton

Troy

Tru ro

Try on

Tuck er ton

Tuf ton burg

Tul ly

Tun bridge

Tur bet

Tur key

Turn er

Twig twees

Tyngs burg

Tyr ing ham

Tyr rel

U

Uls ter

Un der hill

U ni on

U ni ty

Up ton

U ti ca

U trecht

Ux bridge

V

Vas sal burg

Veal town

Ver non

Ver shire

Vic to ry

Vin cent

Vir gil

Vol un town

W

Wades burg

Wad me law

Wads worth

Wad ham

Waits field

Wa jo mic

Wake field

Wak a maw

Wal den

Wald burg

Wales

Wal ling ford

Wall kill

Wall pack

Wal pole

Wal sing ham

Walt ham

Wand o

Want age

Wards burg

Wards bridge

Ware

Ware ham

War min ster

Warn er

War ren

War ren ton

War ring ton

War saw

War wick

Wash ing ton

Wa ter burg

Wa ter bu ry

Wa ter ford

Wa ter town

Wa ter vliet

Waw a sink

Wayne

Waynes burg

Weare

Weth ers field

Wei sen berg

Well fleet

Wells

Wen dell

Wen ham

Went worth

We sel

West bo rough

Wes ter ly

Wes tern

West field

West ford

West ham

West min ster

West more

West more land

West on

West port

West town

Wey mouth

Wey bridge

Whar ton

Whate ly

Wheel ing

Whee lock

Whip pa ny

White field

White marsh

Whit paine

White plains

Whites town

Whi ting

Whit ting ham

Wick ford

Wil bra ham

Wilks bar re

Will iams burg

Will iams port

Will iam son

Will iams town

Wil lin burg

Wil ling ton

Wil lis

Wil lis ton

Wills burg

Wil man ton

Wil ming ton

Wil mot

Wil son ville

Win chen don

Win ches ter
Wind ham
Win hall
Win lock
Win ni pec
Winns burg
Wins low
Win ter ham
Win throp
Win ton
Wo burn
Wol cott

Wolf burg
Wo mel dorf
Wood bridge
Wood bu ry
Wood creek
Wood ford
Wood stock
Woods town
Wool wich
Worces ter
Wor thing ton
Wrent ham

Wrights burg
Wrights town
Wy an dots
Wyn ton
Wythe

Y
Yad kin
Yar mouth
Yonk ers
York
York town

The following have the accent on the second syllable.

A
A bac´ co
A bit i bis
A ca di a
A quac nac
A las ka
Al gon kins
Al kan sas
A me lia
A me ni a
An co cus
A run del
An til les
An to ni o
A pu ri ma
A quid nec
Ash cut ney
As sin i boin
As sump tion
Au re li us
Au ro ra

B
Bald ea gle
Bal div i a
Ba leze

Bark ham sted
Bar thol o mew
Bel laire
Bell grove
Bel pre
Ber bice
Ber mu da
Ber tie
Bil ler i ca
Bo quet
Bos caw en
Brook ha ven

C
Ca bar rus
Co han sie
Ca ho ki a
Ca mil lus
Cam peach y
Caer nar von
Co nan i cut
Ca rac as
Ca ran gas
Car lisle
Cas tine
Ca taw ba
Ca val lo

Cay lo ma
Cay enne
Caz no vi a
Cham blee
Char lo tia
Che buc to
Che mung
Che raws
Chi a pa
Chop tank
Chow an
Cler mont
Chi ca go
Co do rus
Co chel mus
Co col i co
Co che cho
Cock sa kie
Co hoc sink
Co han zy
Co has set
Co hoze
Cole rain
Co lum bi a
Co ne sus
Con hoe ton
Co hos

Coo saw
Cor dil le ras
Corn wal lis
Coo dras
Cow e tas
Cu ma na

D
Daw fus ky
De fi ance
De troit
Din wid die
Do min go
Du anes burg
Dum fries
Dun bar ton
Du page
Du plin

E
E liz a beth
E liz a beth town
Em maus
Eu phra ta
Es cam bi a
Eu sta tia
E so pus
Ex u ma

F
Fair ha ven
Fay ette
Fitz will iam
Flat bush
Flu van na

G
Ge ne va
Ge rards town
Go naives
Gwyn nedd
Graves end
Green bush

Guild hall

H
Ha van na
Hel e na
Hen lo pen
Hi was see
Hon du ras

J
Jac mal
Je ru sa lem

K
Kas kas ki a
Kow sa ki
Key wa wa
Kil lis ti noe
Kil ken ny
King sess ing
Kin sale
Kas kas kunk

L
La com ic
La co ni a
La goon
Le noir
Long bay
Long i sland
Long lake
Long mead ow
Lo ren zo
Lo ret to
Lou i sa
Low hill
Lu cay a
Lu cia
Lu zerne
Ly com ing
Lynn ha ven
Ly san der

M
Ma chi as
Ma cun gy
Ma con nels burg
Ma de ra
Ma hack a mac
Ma ho ney
Ma hone
Ma ho ning
Ma nal lin
Man hat tan
Ma nil lon
Ma quoit
Mar cel lus
Mar gal la way
Ma tane
Ma tan zas
Ma til da
Ma tin i cus
Mat tap o ny
Me dun cook
Me her rin
Mem ram cook
Men do za
Men ol o pen
Me thu en
Mi am i
Mis sisk o
Mine head
Mo bill
Mo he gan
Mo hic con
Mo nad noc
Mon he gan
Mo noc a sy
Mon seag
Mon tauk
Mon te go
Mont gom e ry
Mont pe lier
Mont ville
Mo rant
Mor gan za

Mo shan non
Mul he gan
Musk ing um

N
Na hant
Na mask et
Nan task et
Nan tuck et
Nan tux et
Na shon
Nas keag
Na varre
Ne pon set
Ne sham o ny*
New cas tle
New Eng land
New fane
New paltz
New Roch elle
New U trecht
Ni ag a ra
Ni pis sing
North amp ton
North cas tle
North east
North um ber land

O
Oak fus ky
Oak mul gy
O co ny
O nei da
Or chil la
Os we go
Ot se go
O was co
O we go
O wy hee

P
Pal my ra
Pa munk y
Pa nu co
Pa rai ba
Pas sump sic
Pa taps co
Pa tuck et
Pa tux et
Pau tuck et
Pau tux et
Pe gun noc
Pe jep scot
Pe quon uc
Per a mus
Per cip a ny
Per nam bu co
Perth am boy
Phi lop o lis
Py an ke tunk
Py an ke shaws
Pier mont
Pin chin a
Pi o ri as
Pla cen tia
Po kon ca
Po soom suc
Port roy al
Port penn
Po to si
Pough keep sie
Pound ridge
Presque isle
Pre sums cot
Pro tect worth

Q
Quam pea gan

R
Red hook
Re ho both
Ri van na
Rock on ca ma
Ros seau
Ro siers
Row an

S
Sag har bour
Salt ash
San dus ky
Sa rec to
Sa vil la
Sa voy
Sco har rie
Scow he gan
Se kon net
Se ba go
Se bas ti cook
Se bas tian
Sem pro ni us
Se wee
Sha wan gunk**
Shaw sheen
She nan go
She tuck et
Sche nec ta dy
Skip pac
South amp ton
South hold
Stra bane
Swan na no
Swa ta ra

T
Tap pan

* Pronounced, Shammony.

**Pronounced, Shongum

Ta ba go
Ta bas co
Ta con net
Ta doo sac
Ta en sa
Tar pau lin
Ta wan dy
Ta wixt wy
Ti o ga
To mis ca ning
Tor bay
To ron to
Tor tu gas
Tou lon
Tre coth ic
Trux il lo

Tunk han noc
Ty bee
Ty rone

U
U lys ses
Ur ban na

V
Ver gennes
Ver sailles
Ve nan go

W
Wa cho vi a
Wa chu set

Wal hold ing
Wap pac a mo
Wa tau ga
Wa keag
Web ham et
West chest er
West hamp ton
West In dies
West point
Wi com i co
Wi mac o mac
Win eask
Wi nee
Win yaw
Wis cas set
Wy o ming

The following have the accent on the third syllable, and most of them a secondary accent on the first.

A
Ab be ville´
Ac a pul co
Ac co mac
Ag a men tic us
Ag a mun tic
Al a bam a
Al a chu a
Al be marl
Al le mand
Al va ra do
Am a zo ni a
Am o noo suc
Am us keag
An ah uac
An as ta sia
An ti cos ti
Ap a lach i an
Ap a lach es
Ap o quen e my
Ap po mat ox
A que doch ton

Arch i pel a go
Au gus tine

B
Bas ken ridge
Bel vi dere
Bag a duce
Beth a ba ra
Bux a loons

C
Cach i may o
Cagh ne wa ga
Cal e do ni a
Can a dar qua
Can a wisk
Can i co de o
Car ib bee
Car i coo
Car i boo
Car tha ge na
Cat a ra qua

Cat a wis sa
Cat te hunk
Chab a quid ic
Char le mont
Chat a ho chy
Chat a nu ga
Cher o kee
Chet i ma chas
Chic ca mog ga
Chick a hom i ny
Chick a ma ges
Chick a saw
Chil ho wee
Chil lis quac
Chim bo ra zo
Chris ti an a
Clar e mont
Cin cin na tus
Con a wa go
Con a wan go
Con dus keag
Con e dog we net

Co ne maugh
Cock a la mus
Con es te o
Con es to go
Con ga ree
Coo sa hatch
Co to pax i
Cur ri tuc
Cus co wil la
Cus se wa go

D
Dem e ra ra
Des e a da
E
Eb en e zer
En o ree
Es ca ta ri
Es se que bo
F
Fron ti nac
Freid en huet ten

G
Gal li op o lis
Gen ne see
Gen e vieve
Grad en huet ten

I
In di an a

K
Kar a tunk
Kas ki nom pa
Kay da ros so ra
Ken ne bunk
Kick a poo
Kin der hook
Kis ke man i tas
Kit ta ning
Kit ta tin ny

L
Lach a wan na
Lech a wax en
Let ter ken ny
Lit tle comp ton

M
Mach a noy
Mag da le na
Mag e gad a vie
Ma gel lan
Ma gel la ni a
Mar a cai bo
Man a han
Mar ble head
Mar cus hook
Mar ga ret ta
Ma ri et ta
Mas sa nu ten
Mau re pas
Mel a was ka
Mem fre ma gog
Mack i naw
Mi ro goane
Mis sin abe
Mis si quash
Mo hon ton go
Mo non ga lia
Mont re al
Mor ris se na
Moy a men sing
Mus ko gee

N
Na hun keag
Nan se mond
Nau do wes sy
Nic a ra gua
Nip e gon
Niv er nois
Nock a mix on
Nol a chuc ky

O
Oc co chap po
Oc co neach y
Oc co quan
Oc to ra ro
On a lash ka
Os sa baw
Os we gach y
Ot o gam ies

P
Pak a nok it
Pan a ma
Pan i mar i bo
Pas ca go la
Pas quo tank
Pas sy unk
Pat a go ni a
Pem a quid
Pen sa co la
Per qui mins
Per ki o men
Pitts syl va ni a
Pluck e min
Po ca hon tas
Po co moke
Pont char train
Por to bel lo
Port to bac co
Put a wat o mie

Q
Quem a ho nin

R
Reg o lets
Ri ver head
Rock e mo ko

S
Sag a mond
Sag a naum
Sag en da go

Sal va dore
Sar a nac
Sar a to ga
Sax e go tha
Scat e cook
Seb a cook
Sem i noles
Sin e pux ent
Scan e at e tes
Soc an da ga
Spot syl va ni a
Sur i nam

T

Tal la see
Tal a poo sy
Tap pa han no
The a kik i
Tib e ron
Tow a men sir
To ne wan to
To to wa
Tuck a hoc
Tu cu man
Tul pe hock en
Tus ca ro ra

U

U na dil la
Ui nal ha ven

W
Wah que tank
Wil li man tic
Win ne ba go
Wy a lu sing
Wy a lux ing
Wy o noke

Y
Yu ca tan
Yoh o ga ny

The following are accented on the fourth syllable.

Can a jo har ry
Can a se ra ga
Can e de ra go
Chick a ma com i co
Cob bes e con ty
Co hon go ron to
Con e go cheag

Dam e ris cot ta
Eas tan al lee
Kish a co quil las
Mish il li mack a nac*
Mo non ga he la
Om pom pa noo suc
Pas sam a quod dy

Pem i ge was set
Quin sig a mond
Rip pa ca noe
Sag a da hoc
Sax a pa haw
Ti con de ro ga
Wa nas pe tuck et

*The popular prononuncition of Mishillmackinac.

Islands of the West Indies.

An guil´ la
An ti´ gua[1]
Ba ha´ ma
Ber mu´ da
Bar ba´ does
Bar bu´ da
Cur a so´
Cu´ ba
Dom in i´ co[2]
Mar tin i´ co[3]

Por to ri´ co[4]
Eu sta´ tia
Gre na´ da
Gau da lou´pe[5]
Hai´ ti or
His pan i o´ la
Ja ma´i ca
Mar i ga lant´
Miq ue lon´
Mont ser rat´

Ne´ vis
To ba´ go
Trin i dad´
Sant a Cruse
St. Christ´ o phers
St. Lu cia[6]
St. Mar´ tins
St. Thom´ as
St. Vin´ cent

[1] Pronounced Antega. [2] Domineke. [3] Martineke [4] Portorekeo. [5] Guadaloop. [6] Saint Luzee.

TABLE LII.

OF NUMBERS

Figures. Adjectives.	Letters.	Names.	Numerical
1	I	one	first
2	II	two	second
3	III	three	third
4	IV	four	fourth
5	V	five	fifth
6	VI	six	sixth
7	VII	seven	seventh
8	VIII	eight	eighth
9	IX	nine	ninth
10	X	ten	tenth
11	XI	eleven	eleventh
12	XII	twelve	twelfth
13	XIII	thirteen	thirteenth
14	XIV	fourteen	fourteenth
15	XV	fifteen	fifteenth
16	XVI	sixteen	sixteenth
17	XVII	seventeen	seventeenth
18	XVIII	eighteen	eighteenth
19	XIX	nineteen	nineteenth
20	XX	twenty	twentieth
30	XXX	thirty	thirtieth
40	XL	forty	fortieth
50	L	fifty	fiftieth
60	LX	sixty	sixtieth
70	LXX	seventy	seventieth
80	LXXX	eighty	eightieth
90	XC	ninety	ninetieth
100	C	one hundred	one hundredth
200	CC	two hundred	two hundredth
300	CCC	three hundred	three hundredth
400	CCCC	four hundred	four hundredth
500	D	five hundred	five hundredth
600	DC	six hundred	six hundredth
700	DCC	seven hundred	seven hundredth
800	DCCC	eight hundred	eight hundredth
900	DCCCC	nine hundred	nine hundredth
1000	M	one thousand, &c.	one thousandth
1804	MDCCCIV	one thousand eight-	hundred & four

TABLE LIII.

Words of the same sound, but different in spelling and signification.

Ail – to be troubled
Ale – malt liquor

Air – an element
Are – plural
Heir – to an estate

All – the whole
Awl – an instrument

Al tar – for sacrifice
Al ter – to change

Ant – a pismire
Aunt – uncle's wife

As cent – steepness
As sent – an agreement

Au ger – an instrument
Au gur – one who fortells

Bail – surety
Bale – a pack of goods

Ball – a round substance
Bawl – to cry aloud

Bare – naked
Bear – to suffer
Bear – a beast

Base – vile
Bass – in music
Beer – a liquor
Bier – to carry the dead

Ber ry – a small fruit
Bu ry – to inter the dead

Beat – to strike
Beet – a root

Blew – did blow
Blue – color

Boar – a male swine
Bore – to make a hole

Bow – to bend
Bough – a branch
Bow – to shoot with
Beau – a gay fellow

Bred – brought up
Bread – food

Bur row – for rabbits
Bo rough – a town
corporate

By – a particle
Buy – to purchase

Cain – a man's name
Cane – a shrub or staff

Call – to cry out
Caul – of a wig or bowels

Can non – a large gun
Can on – a rule

Can vass – to examine
Can vas – coarse cloth

Ceil ing – of a room
Seal ing – setting of a seal

Cell – a hut
Sell – to dispose of

Cen tu ry – a hundred years
Cen tau ry – an herb

Chol er – wrath
Col lar – for the neck

Cord – a small rope
Chord – in music

Ci on – a young shoot
Si on – a mountain

Cite – to summon
Sight – seeing
Site – situation

Chron i cal – of a long
   continuance
Chron i cle – a history

Course – order or direction
Coarse – not fine

Com ple ment – full
number
Com pli ment – expression
of civility

Cous in – a relation
Coz en – to cheat

Coun cil – an assembly
Coun sel – advice

Cur rant – a berry
Cur rent – passing, or a
stream

Deer – a wild animal
Dear – of great price

Dew – from heaven
Due – owed

Die – to expire
Dye – to color

Doe – a female deer
Dough – bread unbaked

Dun – brown color
Done – performed

Fane – a weather cock
Fain – gladly
Feign – to dissemble

Faint – weary
Feint – a false march

Fair – comely
Fare – food,
customary duty,
  &c.

Fel lon – a whitlow
Fel on – a criminal

Flea – an insect
Flee – to run away

Flour – of wheat
Flow er – of the field

Fourth – in number
Forth – abroad

Foul – nasty
Fowl – a bird

Gilt – with gold
Guilt – crime
Grate – for coals
Great – large

Groan – to sigh
Grown – increased

Hail – to salute, or frozen
  drops of rain
Hale – sound, healthy

Hart – a beast
Heart – the seat of life

Hare – an animal
Hair – of the head

Here – in this place
Hear – to hearken

Hew – to cut
Hue – color

Him – that man
Hymn – a sacred song
Hire – wages
High er – more high

Heel – of the foot
Heal – to cure

I – myself
Eye – organ of sight

Isle – an island
Aisle – of a church

In – within
Inn – a tavern

In dite – to compose
In dict – to prosecute

Kill – to slay
Kiln – of brick

Knave – a dishonest man
Nave – of a wheel

Knight – by honor
Night – the evening

Know – to be acquainted
No – not so

Knew – did know
New – not old

Knot – made by tying
Not – denying

Lade – to dip water
Laid – placed

Lain – did lie
Lane – a narrow passage

Leek – a root
Leak – to run out

Les son – a reading
Les sen – to diminish

Li ar – a teller of lies
Lyre – a harp

Led – did lead
Lead – heavy metal

Lie – a falsehood, also to
  rest on a bed
Lye – water
drained through ashes

Lo – behold
Low – humble

Made – finished
Maid – an
unmarried woman

Main – the chief
Mane – of a horse

Male – the he kind
Mail – armor, or a packet

Man ner – mode or custom
Man or – a lordship

Meet – to come together
Meat – flesh
Mete – measure

Mite – an insect
Might – strength

Met al -gold or silver, &c.
Met tle – briskness

Naught – bad
Nought – none

Nay – no
Neigh – as a horse

Oar – to row with
Ore – metal not separated

Oh – alas
Owe – to be indebted

One – in number
Won – past time of win

Our – belonging
Hour – sixty minutes

Pale – wanting color
Pail – a vessel

Pain – torment
Pane – a square of glass

Peel – the outside
Peal – upon the bells

Pear – a fruit
Pare – to cut off

Plain – even, or level
Plane – to make smooth

Plate – a flat piece of metal
Plait – a fold in a garment

Pray – to implore
Prey – a booty

Prin ci pal – chief
Prin ci ple – first rule

Proph et – a foreteller
Prof it – advantage

Peace – tranquility
Piece – a part

Rain – falling water
Rein – of a bridle
Reign – to rule

Reed – a shrub
Read – to peruse

Rest – ease
Wrest – to force

Rice – a sort of corn
Rise – origin

Rye – a sort of grain
Wry – crooked

Ring – to sound
Wring – to twist

Rite – ceremony
Right – just
Write – to form letters
  with a pen
Wright – a workman
Rode – did ride
Road – the highway

Roe – a deer
Row – a rank

Ruff – a neckcloth
Rough – not smooth

Sail – of a ship
Sale – a selling

Seen – beheld
Scene – of a stage

See – to behold
Sea – the ocean

Sent – ordered away
Scent – smell

Sen ior – elder
Seign or – a lord

Shore – a side of a river
Shoar – a prop

Sink – to go down
Cinque – five

So – thus
Sow – to scatter

Sum – the whole
Some – a part

Sun – the fountain of light
Son – a male child

Sore – an ulcer
Soar – to mount up

Stare – to look earnestly
Stair – a step

Steel – hard metal
Steal – to take without
lierty

Suc cor – help
Suck er – a young twig

Sleight – dexterity
Slight – to despise

Sole – of the foot
Soul – the spirit

Tax – a rate
Tacks – small nails

Tale – a story
Tail – the end

Tare – weight allowed
Tear – to rend

Team – of cattle or horses
Teem – to go with young

Their – belonging to them
There – in that place

The – a particle
Thee – yourself

Too – likewise
Two – twice one

Tow – to drag after
Toe – of the foot

Vale – a valley
Veil – a covering

Vein – for the blood
Vane – to shew the course
  of the wind

Vice – sin
Vise – a screw

Wait – to tarry
Weight – heaviness

Wear – to put on
Ware – merchandise
Were – past time plural
of am

Waste – to spend
Waist – the middle

Way – road
Weigh – to poise

Week – seven days
Weak – not strong

Wood – trees
Would – was willing

You – plural of thee
Yew – a tree

TABLE LIV.

Of ABBREVIATIONS.

A.A.S. - Fellow of the American Academy
C.A.S. - Fellow of the Connecticut Academy
A.B. - Bachelor of Arts
A.D. - In the year of our Lord
A.M. - Master of Arts, before noon, or in the year of the world
Bart. - Baronet
B.D. - Bachelor of Divinity
C. or Cent. - an hundred
Capt. - Captain
Col. - Colonel
Cant. - Canticles
Chap. - Chapter
Chron. - Chronicles
Co. - Company
Com. - Commissioner
Cr. - Credit
Dwt. - Hundred weight
D.D. - Doctor of Divinity
Dr. - Doctor or Debtor
Dec. - December
Dep. - Deputy
Deut. - Deuteronomy
Do. or ditto – the same
E.G. - for example
Eccl. - Ecclesiastes
Ep. - Epistle
Eng. - English
Eph. - Ephesians
Esa. - Esaias
Ex. - Example, or Exodus
Feb. - February
Fr. - France, or Francis
F.R.S. - Fellow of the Royal
Society
Gal. - Galatians
Gen. - Genesis
Gent. - Gentleman
Geo. - George
G.R. - George the King
Heb. - Hebrews
Hon. - Honorable
Hund. - Hundred
Ibidem, ibid. - in the same place
Isa. - Isaiah
i.e. - that is
Id. - the same
Jan. - January
Ja. - James
Jac. - Jacob
Josh. - Joshua
K. - King
Km. - Kingdom
Kt. - Knight
L. - Lord or Lady
Lev. - Leviticus
Lieut. - Lieutenant
L.L.D. - Doctor of Laws
L.S – the place of the Seal
Lond. - London
M. - Marquis
M.B. - Bachelor of Physics
Mr. - Master
Messrs. - Gentlemen, Sirs
Mrs. - Mistress
M.S. - Manuscript
M.S.S. - Manuscripts
Mat. - Mathew
Math – Mathematics
N.B. - take particular notice
Nov. - November

No. - Number
N.S. - New Style
Obj. - Objection
Oct. - October
O.S. - Old Style
Parl. - Parliament
Per cent. - by the hundred
Pet. - Peter
Phil. - Philip
Philom. - a lover of learning
P.M. - Afternoon
P.S. - Postscript
Ps. - Psalm
Q. - Question, Queen
q.d. - as if he should say
q.l. - as much as you please
Regr. - Register
Rev. - Revelation, Reverend

Rt. Hon. - Right Honorable
S. - South and Shilling
St. - Saint
Sept. - September
Serj. - Sergeant
S.T.P. - Professor of Divinity
S.T.D. - Doctor of Divinity
ss. - to wit, namely
Theo. - Theophilus
Tho. - Thomas
Thess. - Thessalonians
V. - or vide, see
Viz. - to wit, namely
Wm. - William
Wp. - Worship
& - and
&c. - and so forth
U.S.A. - United States of America

EXPLANATION

Of the PAUSES and other CHARACTERS used in WRITING.

A comma (,) is a pause of one syllable; A semicolon (;) two; A colon (:) four; A period (.) six; An interrogation point (?) shows when a question is asked; as, What do you see? An exclamation point (!) is a mark of wonder or surprise; as, O the folly of sinners! The pause of these two points is the same as a colon or a period, and the sentence should usually be closed with a raised tone of voice.

( ) A parenthesis includes a part of a sentence, which is not necessary to make sense, and should be read quicker, and in a weaker tone of voice.

[ ] Brackets or Hooks, include words that serve to explain a foregoing word or sentence.

- A Hyphen joins words or syllables; as, sea-water.

‘ An Apostrophe shows when a letter is omitted, as us’d for used.

^ A Caret shows when a word or number of words are

my

omitted through mistake; as, this is ^ book.

"A quotation or double comma, includes a passage that is taken from some other author in his own words.

☞ The index, points to some remarkable passage.

¶ The Paragraph begins a new subject.

§ The Section is used to divide chapters.

*†‡ An Asterisk, and other references, point to a note in the margin or bottom of a page.

OF CAPITAL LETTERS.

Sentences should begin with a capital letter; also every line in poetry. Proper names, which are the names of persons, places, rivers, mountains, lakes, &c. should begin with a capital. Also the name of the Supreme Being.

ADDITIONAL LESSONS

DOMESTIC ECONOMY

Or, The History of THRIFTY and UNTHRIFTY.

THERE is a great difference among men, in their ability to gain property; but a still greater difference in their power of using it to advantage. Two men may acquire the same amount of money, in a given time; yet one will prove to be a poor man, while the other becomes rich. A chief and essential difference in the management of property, is, that one man spends only the interest of his money, while another spends the principal.

I know a farmer by the name of THRIFTY, who manages his affairs in this manner: He rises early in the morning, looks to the condition of his house, barn, home-lot and stock,sees that his cattle, horses and hogs are fed; examines the tools to see whether they are all in good order for the workmen; takes care that breakfast is ready in due season, and begins work in the cool of the day. When in the field, he keeps steadily at work, though not so violently as to fatigue and exhaust the body; nor does he stop to tell or hear long stories. When the labor of the day is past, he takes refreshment, and goes to rest at an early hour. In this manner he earns and gains money.

When Thrifty has acquired a little property, he does not spend it or let it slip from him, without use or benefit. He pays his taxes and debts when due or called for, so that he has no officers fees to pay, nor expenses of courts. He does not frequent the tavern and drink up all his earnings in liquor that does him no good. He puts his money to use, that is, he buys more land, or stock, or lends his money at interest – in short, he makes his money produce some profit or income. These savings and profits, though small by themselves, amount in a year to a considerable sum, and in a few years, they swell to an estate – Thrifty becomes a wealthy farmer, with several hundred acres of land, and a hundred head of cattle.

Very different is the management of UNTHRIFTY: He lies in bed, till a late hour, in the morning; then rises, and goes to the bottle for a dram, or to the tavern for a glass of bitters. Thus he spends six cents before breakfast, for a dram that makes him dull and heavy all day. He gets his breakfast late, when he ought to be at work. When he supposes he is ready to begin the work of the day, he finds he has not the necessary tools, or some of them are out of order, – the plow-share is to be sent half a mile to a blacksmith to be mended; a tooth or two in a rake or the handle of a hoe, is broke; or a scythe or an ax is to be ground. Now, he is in a great hurry; he bustles about to make preparation for work – and what is done in a hurry is ill done. He loses a part of the day in getting ready – and perhaps the time of his workmen. At ten or eleven o'clock he is ready to go to work. Then comes a boy and tells him, the sheep have escaped from the pasture, or the cows have got among his corn, or the hogs into the garden. He frets and storms, and runs to drive them out. A half hour or more time is lost in driving the cattle from mischief, and repairing a poor broken fence – a fence that answers no purpose but to lull him into security, and teach his horses and cattle to be unruly. After all this bustle, the fatigue of which is worse than common labor, Unthrifty is ready to begin a day's work at twelve o'clock. Thus half his time is lost in supplying defects, which proceed from want of foresight and good management. His small crops are damaged or destroyed by unruly cattle. His barn is open and leaky, and what little he gathers, is injured by the rain and snow. His house is in a like condition – the shingles and clapboards fall off and let in the water, which caused the timber, floors and furniture to decay – and exposed to inclemencies of weather, his wife and children fall sick – their time is lost, and the mischief closes with a ruinous train of expenses for medicines and physicians. After dragging out some years of disappointment, misery and poverty, the lawyer and the sheriff sweep away the scanty remains of his estate. This is the history of UNTHRIFTY – his principal is spent – he has no interest.

Not unlike this, is the history of the Grog-drinker. This man wonders why he does not thrive in the world; he cannot see the reason why his neighbor Temperance should be more prosperous than himself – but in truth, he makes no calculations. Ten cents a day for grog, is a small sum, he thinks, which can hurt no man! But let us make an estimate – arithmetic is very useful for a man who ventures to spend small sums every day. Ten cents a day amount in a year to thirty-six dollars and a half – a sum sufficient to buy a good farm horse! This surely is no small sum for a farmer or mechanic. But in ten years, this sum amounts to three hundred and sixty five dollars, besides interest in the mean time! What an amount is this for drams and bitters in ten years! It is money enough to build a small house! But look at the amount in thirty years! One thousand and ninety five dollars! What a vast sum to run down one man's throat in liquor – a sum that will buy a farm sufficient to maintain a small family. Suppose a family to consume a quart of spirits in a day, at twenty-five cents a quart. The amount of this in a year, is ninety-one dollars and a quarter; in ten years, nine hundred and twelve dollars and a half; and in thirty years, two thousand, seven hundred and thirty-seven dollars and a half! A great estate, may thus be consumed, in single quarts of rum! What mischief is done by the love of spirituous liquors!

"But," says the laboring man, "I cannot work without spirits – I must have something to give me strength." Then drink something that will give durable nourishment. Of all the substances taken into the stomach, spirituous liquors contain the least nutriment, and add the least to bodily vigor. Malt liquors, molasses and water, milk and water, contain nutriment, and even cider is not wholly destitute of it – but distilled spirituous liquors contain little or none.

"But," says the laborer or the traveler, "spirituous liquors warm the stomach, and are very useful in cold weather." No, this is not correct. Spirits enliven the feelings for half an hour – but leave the body more dull, languid and cold than it was before. A man will freeze the sooner for drinking spirits of any kind. If a man wishes to guard against cold, let him eat a biscuit, a bit of bread or a meal of victuals. Four ounces of bread will give a more durable warmth to the body, than a gallon of spirits – food is the natural stimulant or exciting power of the human body – it gives warmth and strength, and does not leave the body, as spirit does, more feeble and languid. The practice of drinking spirits gives a man red eyes, a bloated face, and an empty purse. It injures the liver, produces dropsy, occasions a trembling of the joints and limbs, and closes life with a slow decay or palsy – this is a short history of the drinker of distilled spirits. If a few drinking men are found to be exceptions to this account, still the remarks are true, as they apply to most cases. Spirituous liquors shorten more lives than famine, pestilence and the sword!

LESSONS ON FAMILIAR SUBJECTS.

All mankind live on the fruits of the earth – the first and most necessary employment therefore is the tillage of the ground, called agriculture, husbandry, or farming.

The farmer clears his land of trees, roots and stones. He surrounds it with a fence of poles, posts and rails, stone-wall, hedge or ditch. He plows and harrows, or drags the soil, to break the clods or turf, and make it mellow and pliable. He manures it also, if necessary, with stable dung, ashes, marl, plaster, lime, sea-shells, or decayed vegetable substances. He plants maize in rows, or sows wheat, barley, rye, oats, buckwheat, flax or hemp. He hoes the maize, two or three times, kills the weeds and draws the earth round the hills to support and nourish the plants. When the grain is ripe, he reaps or cradles his grain, and pulls the flax. The ears of maize are picked by hand, or the stalks cut with a sickle or knife and the husks are stripped off, in the evening. With what joy does the farmer gather his crops, of the former and latter harvest! He toils indeed, but he reaps the fruit of his labor in peace – he fills his granary in summer, and in autumn presents a thank-offering to God for his bounty.

See the mower, how he swings his scythe! The grass falls prostrate before him – the glory of the field is laid low – the land is stripped of its verdant covering. See the stripling follow his father or brother and with a pitch fork, spread the thick swath, and shake the grass about the meadow! How fragrant the smell of new made hay – how delightful the task to tend it!

Enter the forest of the wilderness. See here and there a rustic dwelling made of logs – a little spot cleared and cultivated – a thatched hovel to shelter a cow and her food – the forest resounding with the ax-man's blows, as he levels the sturdy beach, maple, or hemlock; while the crackling fire aids his hands, by consuming the massy piles of wood which he cannot remove. Hear the howling wolf, or watch the nimble deer, as he bounds along among the trees. The faithful cow, in search of shrubs and twigs, strays from the cottage, and the owner seeks her at evening, in the gloomy forest; led by the tinkling of the bell, he finds and drives her home. A bowl of bread and milk furnishes him with his frugal repast; he retires weary to rest – and the sleep of the laboring man is sweet.

See the dairy woman, while she fills her pails with new milk – the gentle cows quietly chewing their cuds by her side. Enter the milk-room, see the pans, pails and tubs, how clean and sweet, all in order, and fit for use! The milk strained and put in a cool place – the cream skimmed off for butter, or the milk set for cheese. Here is a churn as white as ivory – there a cheese-press forcing the whey from the curd! See the shelves filled with cheeses. What a noble sight! And butter as yellow as the purest gold!

George, let us look into the work-shops among the mechanics. Here is a carpenter, he squares a post or a beam; he scores or notches it first, and then hews it with his broad-ax. He bores holes with an auger, and with the help of a chisel forms a mortise for a tenon. He measures with a square or rule, and marks his work with a compass. Each timber is fitted to its place. The sills support the posts, and these support the beams. Braces secure the frame of a building from swaying or leaning. Girders and joists support the floors; studs, with the posts, support the walls, and the rafters uphold the roof.

Now comes the joiner with his chest of tools. He plains the boards, joints the shingles, and covers the building. With his saw he cuts boards, with his gimblet or whimble, he makes holes for nails, pins or spikes; with his chisel and gouge, he makes mortises.

Then comes the mason with his trowel. The laths are nailed to the studs and joists to support the plaster. First a rough coat of coarse mortar of lime and sand is laid on, and this is covered with a beautiful white plaster. And last of all comes the painter with his brush and oil-pots. He mixes the oil and white lead, and gives to the apartments the color which the owner or his lady sees fit to direct.

A MORAL CATECHISM.

Question. WHAT is moral virtue?

Answer. It is an honest upright conduct in all our deal-ings with men.

Q. What rules have we to direct us in our moral conduct?

A. God's word, contained in the Bible, has furnished all necessary rules to direct our conduct.

Q. In what part of the Bible are these rules to be found?

A. In almost every part; but the most important duties between men are summed up in the beginning of Matthew, in CHRIST'S Sermon on the Mount.

OF HUMILITY.

Q. What is humility?

A. A lowly temper of mind.

Q. What are the advantages of humility?

A. The advantages of humility in this life are very numerous and great. The humble man has few or no enemies. Every one loves him and is ready to do him good. If he is rich and prosperous, people do not envy him; if he is poor and unfortunate, every one pities him, and is disposed to alleviate his distresses.

Q. What is pride?

A. A lofty high minded disposition.

Q. Is pride commendable?

A. By no means. A modest, self approving opinion of our own good deeds is very right – it is natural – it is agreeable, and a spur to good actions. But we should not suffer our hearts to be blown up with pride, whatever great and good deeds we have done; for pride brings upon us the ill-will of mankind, and displeasure of our Maker.

Q. What effect has humility upon our own minds?

A. Humility is attended with peace of mind and self-satisfaction. The humble man is not disturbed with cross accidents, and is never fretful and uneasy; nor does he repine when others grow rich. He is contented, because his mind is at ease.

Q. What is the effect of pride on a man's happiness?

A. Pride exposes a man to numberless disappointments and mortifications. The proud man expects more attention and respect will be paid to him, than he deserves, or than others are willing to pay him. He is neglected, laughed at and despised, and this treatment frets him, so that his own mind becomes a seat of torment. A proud man cannot be a happy man.

Q. What has Christ said, respecting the virtue of humility?

A. He has said, "Blessed are the poor in spirit, for theirs is the kingdom of heaven." Poorness of spirit is humility; and this humble temper prepares a man for heaven, where all is peace and love.

OF MERCY.

Q. What is mercy?

A. It is tenderness of heart.

Q. What are the advantages of this virtue?

A. The exercise of it tends to diffuse happiness and lessen the evils of life. Rulers of a merciful temper will make their good subjects happy, and will not torment the bad with needless severity. Parents and masters will not abuse their children and servants with harsh treatment. More love, more confidence, more happiness, will subsist among men, and of course society will be happier.

Q. Should not beasts as well as men be treated with mercy?

A. They ought indeed. It is wrong to give needless pain even to a beast. Cruelty to the brutes shows a man has a hard heart, and if a man is unfeeling to a beast, he will not have much feeling for men. If a man treats his beast with cruelty, beware of trusting yourself in his power. He will probably make a severe master and a cruel husband.

Q. How does cruelty show its effects?

A. A cruel disposition is usually exercised upon those who are under its power. Cruel rulers make severe laws which injure the persons and properties of their subjects. Cruel officers execute laws in a sever manner, when it is not necessary for public good. A cruel husband abuses his wife and children. A cruel master acts the tyrant over his apprentices and servants. The effects of cruelty are hatred, quarrels, tumults and wretchedness.

Q. What does Christ say of the merciful man?

A. He says he is "blessed, for he shall obtain mercy." He who shows mercy and tenderness to others, will be treated with tenderness and compassion himself.

OF PEACE-MAKERS.

Q. Who are peace-makers?

A. All who endeavor to prevent quarrels and disputes among men; or to reconcile those who are separated by strife.

Q. Is it unlawful to contend with others on any occasion?

A. It is impossible to avoid some differences with men.

OF PURITY OF HEART.

Q. What is a pure heart?

A. A heart free from all bad desires, and inclined to conform to the divine will in all things.

Q. Should a man's intentions as well as his actions be good?

A. Most certainly. Actions cannot be called good, unless they proceed from good motives. We should wish to see and to make all men better and happier – we should rejoice at their prosperity. This is benevolence.

Q. What reward is promised to the pure in heart?

A. Christ has declared "they shall see God." A pure heart is like God, and those who possess it shall dwell in His presence and enjoy His favor for ever.

OF ANGER.

Q. Is it right ever to be angry?

A. It is right in certain cases that we should be angry; as when gross affronts are offered to us, and injuries done us by design. A suitable spirit of resentment, in such cases, will obtain justice for us, and protect us from further insults.

Q. By what rule should anger be governed?

A. We should never be angry without cause; that is, we should be certain that a person means to affront, injure or insult us, before we suffer ourselves to be angry. It is wrong, it is mean, it is a mark of a little mind to take fire at every little trifling dispute. And when we have real cause to be angry, we should observe moderation. We should never be in a passion. A passionate man is like a madman and is always inexcusable. We should be cool even in anger, and be angry no longer than to obtain justice. In short, we should "be angry and sin not."

OF REVENGE.

Q. What is revenge?

A. It is to injure a man because he has injured us.

Q. Is this justifiable?

A. Never, in any possible case. Revenge is perhaps the meanest, as well as the wickedest vice in society.

Q. What shall a man do to obtain justice when he is injured?

A. In general, laws have made provision for doing justice to every man; and it is right and honorable, when a man is injured, that he should seek a recompense. But a recompense is all he can demand, and of that he should not be his own judge, but should submit the matter to judges appointed by authority.

Q. But suppose a man insults us in such a manner that the law cannot give us redress?

A. Then forgive him. "If a man strikes you on one cheek, turn the other to him," and let him repeat the abuse, rather than strike him.

Q. But if we are in danger from the blows of another, may we not defend ourselves?

A. Most certainly. We have always a right to defend our persons, property and families. But we have no right to fight and abuse people merely for revenge. It is nobler to forgive. "Love your enemies; bless them that curse you; do good to them that hate you; pray for them that use you ill," – these are the commands of the blessed Savior of men. The man who does this is great and good; he is as much above the little, mean, revengeful man, as virtue is above vice, or as heaven is higher than hell.

OF JUSTICE.

Q. What is justice?

A. It is giving to every man his due.

Q. Is it always easy to know what is just?

A. It is generally easy; and where there is any difficulty in determining, let a man consult the golden rule – "To do to others, what he could reasonably wish they should do to him, in the same circumstances."

Q. What are the ill effects of injustice?

A. If a man does injustice, or rather, if he refuses to do justice, he must be compelled. Then follows a lawsuit, with a series of expenses, and what is worse, ill-blood and enmity between the parties. Somebody is always the worse for law-suits, and of course society is less happy.

OF GENEROSITY.

Q. What is generosity?

A. It is some act of kindness performed for another which strict justice does not demand.

Q. Is this a virtue?

A. It is indeed a noble virtue. To do justice, is well; but to do more than justice, is still better, and may proceed from nobler motives.

Q. What has Christ said respecting generosity?

A. He has commanded us to be generous in this passage, "Whosoever shall compel (or urge) you to go a mile, go with him two.

Q. Are we to perform this literally?

A. The meaning of this command will not always require this. – But in general we are to do more for others than they ask, provided we can do it, without essentially injuring our-selves. We ought cheerfully to suffer many inconveniences to oblige others, though we are not required to do ourselves any essential injury.

Q. Of what advantage is generosity to the man who exercises it?

A. It lays others under obligations to the generous man; and the probability is, that he will be repaid three-fold. Every man on earth wants favors at some time or other in his life; and if we will not help others, others will not help us. It is for a man's interest to be generous.

Q. Ought we to do kind actions because it is for our interest?

A. This may be a motive at all times; but if it is the principal motive, it is less honorable. We ought to do good as we have opportunity, at all times and to all men, whether we expect a reward or not; for if we do good, somebody is the happier for it. This alone is reason enough, why we should do all the good in our power.

OF GRATITUDE.

Q. What is gratitude?

A. A thankfulness of heart for favors received.

Q. Is it a duty to be thankful for favors?

A. It is a duty and a virtue. A man who does not feel grateful for kind acts done for him by others, does not deserve favors of any kind. He ought to be shut out from the society of the good. He is worse than a savage, for a savage never forgets an act of kindness.

Q. What is the effect of true kindness?

A. It softens the heart towards the generous man, and every thing which subdues the pride and other unsocial passions of the heart, fits a man to be a better citizen, a better neighbor, a better husband and a better friend. A man who is sensible of favors and ready to acknowledge them, is more inclined to perform kind offices, not only towards his benefactor, but towards all others.

OF TRUTH.

Q. What is truth?

A. It is speaking and acting agreeable to fact.

Q. Is it a duty to speak truth at all times?

A. If we speak at all, we should tell the truth. It is not always necessary to tell what we know. There are many things which concern ourselves and others which we had better not publish to the world.

Q. What rules are there respecting the publishing of truth?

A. 1. When we are called upon to testify in court, we should speak the whole truth and that without disguise. To leave out small circumstances, or to give coloring to others, with a view to favor one side more than the other, is to the highest degree criminal.

2. When we know something of our neighbor which is against his character, we may not publish it, unless to prevent his doing an injury to another person.

3. When we sell any thing to another, we ought not to represent the article to be better than it really is. If there are faults in it which may easily be seen, the law of man does not require us to inform the buyer of these faults, because he may see them himself. But it is not honorable nor generous, nor strictly honest to conceal even apparent faults. But when faults are out of sight, the seller ought to tell the buyer of them. If he does not, he is a cheat and a downright knave.

Q. What are the ill effects of lying and deceiving?

A. The man who lies, deceives or cheats, loses his reputa-tion. No person will believe him, even when he speaks the truth; he is shunned as a pest to society.

Falsehood and cheating destroy all confidence between man and man; they raise jealousies and suspicions among men; they thus weaken the bands of society and destroy happiness. Besides, cheating often strips people of their property, and makes them poor and wretched.

OF CHARITY AND GIVING ALMS.

Q. What is charity?

A. It signifies giving to the poor, or it is a favorable opinion of men and their actions.

Q. When and how far is it our duty to give to the poor?

A. When others really want what we can spare without material injury to ourselves, it is our duty to give them something to relieve their wants.

Q. When persons are reduced to want by their own lazi-ness and vices, by drunkenness, gambling and the like, is it a duty to relieve them?

A. In general, it is not. The man who gives money and provisions to a lazy, vicious man, becomes a partaker of his guilt. Perhaps it may be right, to give such a man a meal of victuals to keep him from starving, and it is certainly right to feed his wife and family, and make them comfortable.

Q. Who are the proper objects of charity?

A. Persons who are reduced to want by sickness, un-avoidable losses by fire, storms at sea or land, drouth or ac-cidents of other kinds. To such persons we are commanded to give; and it is our own interest to be charitable; for we are all liable to misfortunes and may want charity ourselves.

Q. In what manner should we bestow favors?

A. We should do it with gentleness and affection; putting on no airs of pride and arrogance. We should also take no pains to publish our charities, but rather to conceal them; for if we boast of our generosity, we discover that we give from mean, selfish motives. Christ commands us, in giving alms, not to let our left hand know what our right hand doeth.

Q. How can charity be exercised in our opinions of others?

A. By thinking favorable of them and their actions. Every man has his faults; but charity will not put a harsh construction on another's conduct. It will not charge his conduct to bad views and motives, unless this appears very clear indeed.

OF AVARICE.

Q. What is avarice?

A. An excessive desire of possessing wealth.

Q. Is this commendable?

A. It is not; but one of the meanest of vices.

Q. Can an avaricious man be an honest man?

A. It is hardly possible; for the lust of gain is almost always accompanied with a disposition to take mean and undue advantages of others.

Q. What effect has avarice upon the heart?

A. It contracts the heart – narrows the sphere of benevo-lence – blunts all the fine feelings of sensibility, and sours the mind towards society. An avaricious man, a miser, a niggard, is wrapped up in selfishness, like some worms, which crawl about and eat for some time to fill themselves, then wind themselves up in separate coverings and die.

Q. What injury is done by avarice to society?

A. Avarice gathers together more property, than the owner wants, and keeps it hoarded up, where it does no good. The poor are thus deprived of some business, some means of support; the property gains nothing to the com-munity; and somebody is less happy by means of this hoarding of wealth.

Q. In what proportion does avarice do hurt?

A. In an exact proportion to its power of doing good. The miser's heart grows less, in proportion as his estate grows larger. The more money he has, the more he has people in his power, and the more he grinds the face of the poor. The larger the tree and the more spreading the branches, the more small plants are shaded and robbed of their nourish-ment.

OF FRUGALITY AND ECONOMY.

Q. What is the distinction between frugality and avarice?

A. Frugality is a prudent saving of property from needless waste. Avarice gathers more and spends less than is necessary.

Q. What is economy?

A. It is frugality in expenses – it is a prudent management of one's estate. It disposes of property for useful purposes without waste.

Q. How far does true economy extend?

A. To the saving of everything which it is not necessary to spend for comfort and convenience; and the keeping one's expenses within his income or earnings.

Q. What is wastefulness?

A. It is the spending of money for what is not wanted. If a man drinks a dram which is not necessary for him, or buys a cane which he does not want, he wastes his money. He injures himself, as much as if he had thrown away his money.

Q. Is not waste often occasioned by mere negligence?

A. Very often. The man who does not keep his house and barn well covered; who does not keep good fences about his fields; who suffers his farming utensils to lie out in the rain or on the ground; or his cattle to waste manure in the high way, is as much a spendthrift as the tavern haunter, the tipler, and the gamester.

Q. Do not careless, slovenly people work harder than the neat and orderly?

A. Much harder. It is more labor to destroy a growth of sturdy weeds, than to pull them up when they first spring from the ground. So the disorders and abuse which grow out of a sloven's carelessness, in time, become almost incurable. Hence such people work like slaves, and to little effect.

OF INDUSTRY.

Q. What is industry?

A. It is a diligent attention to business in our several occupations.

Q. Is labor a curse or a blessing?

A. Hard labor or drudgery is often a curse, by making life toilsome and painful. But constant moderate labor is the greatest of blessings.

Q. Why then do people complain of it?

A. Because they do not know the evils of not laboring. Labor keeps the body in health and makes men relish all their enjoyments. "The sleep of the laboring man is sweet," so is his food. He walks cheerful and whistling about his field or his shop, and scarcely knows pain.

The rich and indolent first lose their health for want of action – They turn pale, their bodies are enfeebled, they lose their appetite for food and sleep, they yawn out a tasteless life of dullness, without pleasure, and often useless to the world.

Q. What are the other good effects of industry?

A. One effect is to procure an estate. Our Creator has kindly united our duty, our interest and happiness for the same labor which makes us healthy and cheerful, gives wealth.

Another good effect of industry is, to keep men from vice. Not all the moral discourses ever delivered mankind, have so much effect in checking the bad passions of men, in keeping order and peace, and maintaining moral virtue in society, as industry. Business is a source of health, of prosperity, of virtue and obedience to law.

To make good subjects and good citizens, the first requi-site is to educate every young person, in some kind of busi-ness. The possession of millions should not excuse a young man from application to business; and that parent or guard-ian who suffers his child or his ward to be bred in idleness, becomes accessary to the vices and disorder of society – He is guilty of "not providing for his household, and is worse than an infidel."

OF CHEERFULNESS.

Q. Is cheerfulness a virtue?

A. It doubtless is, and a moral duty to practice it.

Q. Can we be cheerful when we please?

A. In general it depends much on ourselves. We can often mold our tempers into a cheerful frame. – We can frequent company and other objects calculated to inspire us with cheerfulness. To indulge an habitual gloominess of mind is weakness and sin.

Q. What are the effects of cheerfulness on others?

A. Cheerfulness is readily communicated to others, by which means their happiness is increased. We are all influenced by sympathy, and naturally partake of the joys and sorrows of others.

Q. What effect has melancholy on the heart?

A. It hardens and benums it – It chills the warm affec-tions of love and friendship, and prevents the exercise of the social passions. A melancholy person's life is all night and winter. It is as unnatural as perpetual darkness and frost.

Q. What shall one do when overwhelmed with grief?

A. The best method of expelling grief from the mind, or of quieting its pains, is to change the objects that are about us; to ride from place to place, and frequent cheerful company. It is our duty so to do, especially when grief sits heavy on the heart.

Q. Is it not right to grieve for the loss of our friends?

A. It is certainly right; but we should endeavor to moder-ate our grief, and not suffer it to impair our health, or to grow into a settled melancholy. The use of grief is to soften the heart and make us better. But when our friends are dead, we can render them no further service. Our duty to them ends, when we commit them to the grave; but our duty to ourselves, our families and surviving friends, requires that we perform to them the customary offices of life. We should therefore remember our departed friends only to imitate their virtues; and not to pine away with useless sorrow.

Q. Has not religion a tendency to fill the mind with gloom?

A. True religion never has this effect. Superstition and false notions of God, often make men gloomy; but true, rational piety and religion have the contrary effect. They

fill the mind with joy and cheerfulness; and the countenance of a truly pious man should always wear a serene smile.

Q. What has Christ said concerning gloomy Christians?

A. He has pronounced them hypocrites; and commanded his followers not to copy their sad countenances and dis-figured faces; but even in their acts of humiliation to "anoint their heads and wash their feet." Christ intended by this, that religion does not consist in, nor require a monkish sadness and gravity; on the other hand, he intimates that such appearances of sanctity are generally the marks of hypocrisy. He expressly enjoins upon his followers, marks of cheerfulness. Indeed, the only true ground of perpetual cheerfulness, is, a consciousness of ever having done well, and an assurance of divine favor.

FINIS.

www.ingramcontent.com/pod-product-compliance
Lightning Source LLC
Chambersburg PA
CBHW080556090426
42735CB00016B/3255